MW01515252

PROJECTION FACTORISATIONS IN PARTIAL EVALUATION

Distinguished Dissertations in Computer Science

Edited by
C.J. van Rijsbergen, University of Glasgow

The Conference of Professors of Computer Science (CPCS), in conjunction
with the British Computer Society (BCS), selects annually for publication
up to four of the best British PhD dissertations in computer science. The
scheme began in 1990. Its aim is to make more visible the significant
contribution made by Britain – in particular by students – to computer
science, and to provide a model for future students. Dissertations are selected
on behalf of CPCS by a panel whose members are:

C. A. R. Hoare, University of Oxford
R. J. M. Hughes, University of Glasgow
R. Milner, University of Edinburgh (Chairman)
R. Needham, University of Cambridge
M. S. Paterson, University of Warwick
S. Randell, University of Newcastle
A. Sloman, University of Sussex
F. Sumner, University of Manchester

PROJECTION FACTORISATIONS IN PARTIAL EVALUATION

JOHN LAUNCHBURY
Computing Science Department
Universtity of Glasgow

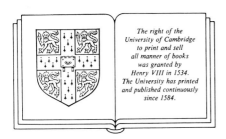

The right of the
University of Cambridge
to print and sell
all manner of books
was granted by
Henry VIII in 1534.
The University has printed
and published continuously
since 1584.

CAMBRIDGE UNIVERSITY PRESS

Cambridge

New York   Port Chester   Melbourne   Sydney

Published by the Press Syndicate of the University of Cambridge
The Pitt Building, Trumpington Street, Cambridge CB2 1RP
40 West 20th Street, New York, NY 10011, USA
10 Stamford Road, Oakleigh, Melbourne 3166, Australia

© Cambridge University Press 1991

First published 1991

Printed in Great Britain at the University Press, Cambridge

Library of Congress cataloguing in publication data available

A catalogue record for this book is available from the British Library

ISBN 0 521 41497 0

Abstract

Partial evaluation is becoming ever more promising as a programming tool. Early partial evaluators depended over much on the source program being written in a particular style, and needed certain *ad hoc* optimisations to produce good results. The practice of partial evaluation is now fairly well developed but the theoretical underpinnings are not equally well understood.

A partial evaluator takes a program, together with some of the input to the program, and produces a new program. This new, or residual, program is an optimised version of the old, having taken the input data into account. Work undertaken at DIKU in Copenhagen has shown the importance of prior analysis of the program. This *binding-time analysis* discovers which values within the program may be computed during partial evaluation (called static values) and which values may not (the dynamic values).

In this thesis we propose using domain projections in binding-time analysis. This allows a greater level of data separation than before because values are no longer treated atomically. In particular, we are able to pinpoint static values within data structures containing both static and dynamic parts. An interesting consequence of using domain projections is that we are able to demonstrate an intimate relationship between binding-time analysis and strictness analysis.

Dependent sum and product are familiar from constructive type theory. We give a less familiar domain-theoretic definition and show how projections determine particular dependent sums. The practical application of this result is to generate residual functions whose types depend on the static values from which they were produced. Certain optimising techniques, such as tag removal and arity raising, arise as a direct consequence.

We extend the use of projections to polymorphic programs, giving a practical application of developments in the theory of polymorphism. Polymorphic functions are regarded as natural transformations between appropriate functors. This leads to three benefits: polymorphic functions are analysed once and the result reused; the static input to polymorphic functions is described by polymorphic projections, which reduces the search space of the analysis; and polymorphic functions are specialised to polymorphic arguments, leading to polymorphic residual functions.

Contents

Preface

This thesis is submitted in partial fulfillment of the requirements for a Doctor of Philosophy Degree at Glasgow University. It comprises a study of partial evaluation, with the thesis that domain projections provide an important theoretical and practical tool for its development.

Our aim, therefore, is not so much to describe a stronger or more robust partial evaluator than has been achieved hitherto, but to improve our understanding of the partial evaluation process. Because of this much of the thesis is theoretical. However, to demonstrate that the ideas are also practical, they have been implemented. As a result, the chapters tend to alternate between theory and practice.

In Chapter 1 we explore the principles of partial evaluation and in Chapter 2 we study the algorithms and techniques used. In Chapters 3 and 4 we address the issue of binding-time analysis. Chapter 3 contains theory, including the relationship between congruence in binding-time analysis and safety in strictness analysis, and Chapter 4 the practice—the equations used in an implementation and a proof of their correctness. In Chapter 5, we discuss the nature of residual functions and their run-time arguments, and develop a theoretical framework based on dependent sums of domains. The practical implications of this are seen in Chapter 6 where we bring the material from the previous chapters together in a working projection-based partial evaluator. In Chapter 7 we turn our attention to polymorphism to address some of the issues it raises, and Chapter 8 concludes the thesis. The appendices which follow contain annotated listings of the programs used to construct the final polymorphic partial evaluator.

To a large extent this thesis is self contained. No prior knowledge of partial evaluation is needed, since a comprehensive introduction is included. However, some knowledge of other areas is assumed, in particular an elementary understanding of both functional languages and domain theory. For Chapters 5 and 7 a little category theory is useful but, again, nothing too deep. In each case appropriate background material may be found in any of the standard references. Bird and Wadler provides an excellent introduction to functional programming [BW88] and Schmidt's chapters on domain theory are very readable [Sch86]. There are few easy introductions to category theory, but both Rydeheard and Burstall [RB88] and Pierce [Pier88] could be recommended. Finally, the reader is encouraged to follow up some of the many excellent references on partial evaluation that are included in the bibliography.

Acknowledgements

This work was funded by a research studentship from the Science and Engineering Research Council, and was undertaken at the Department of Computing Science, Glasgow University. Without the help of many people this thesis would not have been conceived, let alone brought to fruition. I offer my thanks to everyone who has assisted me in whatever way during the last three years and especially to those I name below.

John Hughes has been my supervisor for the duration of my Ph.D. research. He has been a constant source of inspiration and ideas, and his input may be seen throughout the thesis. Thank you John.

Other people at Glasgow also deserve my heartfelt thanks. The department is a very friendly and stimulating place. In particular, the thriving Functional Programming Group is an exciting place to be. Notable among its members is Philip Wadler who has frequently provided me with useful insights.

Going further afield, I must offer my thanks to the MIX group at DIKU in Copenhagen, and in particular to Neil Jones. I have visited DIKU twice during my Ph.D. studies and on both occasions have had very fruitful discussions with the people there. In particular, Neil Jones, Torben Mogensen, Peter Sestoft, Anders Bondorf, Carsten Kehler Holst and Olivier Danvy have all helped me to understand the more intricate aspects of partial evaluation. Peter also deserves thanks for his extensive comments on my first draft.

I wish also to thank Dave Schmidt of Kansas State University, Andrew Pitts of Cambridge University and Michael Johnson of Macquarie University, Sydney, for their patient explanations of areas of domain and category theory.

Returning to Glasgow I would like to thank all my fellow students for our discussions and time together, but in particular Gebre Baraki, Phil Trinder and Steve Blott. On many occasions they listened patiently to half-baked ideas, gently pointing out the areas that were particularly weak.

Other people who deserve particular thanks for the discussions I have had with them are Thierry Coquand, Kieran Clenaghan, Carsten Gomard and Fairouz Kamareddine.

Finally I would like to thank Rachel my wife. She encouraged me whenever I thought I was going nowhere, and cheerfully accepted the times when I spent long periods studying at home or in the department. It is to her that I dedicate this thesis. May God bless her always.

John Launchbury
November 1989

Preface to the Present Edition

In the year or so since I submitted my thesis, various people have drawn my attention to places where the text was poorly worded, or where it contained minor mistakes. In particular, Ryszard Kubiak, and the referees for the Distinguished Dissertation panel have been most helpful in this way. I am indebted to everyone who has taken the trouble to inform me of such shortcomings as I have had the opportunity to perform some limited revision for the present edition.

The most noticeable change from the thesis as originally submitted is the addition of an index. This cross-references all the main ideas of the thesis, and so should facilitate movement around the text.

John Launchbury
February 1991

Chapter 1

Partial Evaluation in Principle

There seems to be a fundamental dichotomy in computing between clarity and efficiency. From the programmer's point of view it is desirable to break a problem into subproblems and to tackle each of the subproblems independently. Once these have been solved the solutions are combined to provide a solution to the original problem. If the decomposition has been well chosen, the final solution will be a clear implementation of the algorithm, but because of intermediate values passing between the various modules, whether they are functions and procedures or separate processes connected by pipes, the solution is unlikely to be as efficient as possible. Conversely, if efficiency is considered paramount, many logically separate computations may need to be performed together. As a consequence, the algorithm will be reflected less directly in the program, and correctness may be hard to ascertain. Thus, in most programs we find a tradeoff between these conflicting requirements of clarity and efficiency.

An extreme form of modularisation is to write programs in an interpretive style, where flow of control is determined by stored data. Programs in this style are comparatively easy to prove correct and to modify when requirements change, but are well known to have extremely poor run-time behaviour—often an order of magnitude slower than their non-interpretive counterparts. Because of this, the interpretive style tends to be used infrequently and in non time-critical contexts. Instead, flow of control is determined deep within the program where a reasonable level of efficiency may be obtained.

Partial evaluation is a serious attempt to tackle this issue. In principle it allows the programmer to write in a heavily interpretive style without paying the corresponding price in efficiency. At *partial evaluation time* (compare with *compile time*) many of the interpretive computations are performed once and for all, and a new program is produced. Flow of control decisions are moved from stored data into the structure of the new program.

Correctness is paramount for partial evaluation to be widely useful. Optimisation phases in many compilers regularly introduce bugs and so are often distrusted by programmers. This is rarely serious because most optimisers may be switched off with little loss—they often give only a marginal improvement anyway. With partial evaluation the situation is very different. In choosing an interpretive style the programmer will be *relying* on the partial evaluation process for making the program reasonably efficient. If the transformation does not preserve the semantics of the source program, then the partial evaluation process cannot be relied upon, and the programmer will return to the original style.

The purpose of this chapter is to survey partial evaluation. Our intention is to provide intuition as to what partial evaluation is and to consider some applications. The name *partial evaluation* is one of a number used to describe the same process. Others are *mixed computation* (because the computation operates on a mix of program text and program data), *program specialisation* (because the new program is a specialised version of the old one), and *program projection* (because in some sense we construct a projection collapsing the first argument).

1.1 Correctness

Let us put all this in a more concrete setting. Suppose we have a program which we intend to run often. Also suppose that for many of the runs some of the input data will remain constant. This means that many of the same computations will be performed repeatedly. We would like to generate a new program from the old one incorporating the data that remains constant. The new program should have the same behaviour when given the remainder of the input as the original did with all the input. Moreover, those computations that would have been performed repeatedly should be performed just once—when the new program is being produced. This latter condition can never be completely satisfied but exists as a goal of partial evaluation. In contrast, the former condition is a requirement that should be satisfied by every partial evaluator. We can express it more formally.

For historical reasons we call our partial evaluator *mix* (from "mixed computation").
Suppose that the program takes two arguments and that we want to specialise it to
its first argument. If we define,

$$\overline{f_x} = mix \ \overline{f} \ \overline{x}$$

then we require that

$$f_x \ y = f \ x \ y$$

The notation we use is intended to draw a distinction between a program and the
function or operation that the program computes. Thus if f is a function, then $\overline{f}$ is
some program defining that function. More generally, if x is a value of any type then $\overline{x}$
is a program (or piece of program text) defining that value. Thus the function *mix* (as
defined by a program $\overline{mix}$) takes two programs as arguments and returns a program
as a result[1]. Similarly, in the example above, $\overline{f_x}$ is a program defining the specialised
function f_x. Notice that this notation does not preclude some non-overlined variable
from having a program value.

We describe the first parameter as *static*. We expect that it will not vary for some
number of runs but, more importantly, its value is known during partial evaluation.
The second parameter, whose value is not known until run-time, is described as
dynamic. Clearly there are natural generalisations of the correctness condition, where
a function may have many parameters, some subset of which are static. One of the
aims of this thesis is to generalise further, so that individual parameters may have
both static and dynamic parts.

1.2 Applications

Partial evaluation has a long history. Lombardi and Raphael used it in LISP to
handle incomplete data [LR64]. Futamura [Fut71] realised that partial evaluation
could be used to derive compilers from interpreters. We will look at his idea in

---

[1]The overbar notation has been introduced here instead of the more common form L mix f x
[JSS85] as it may express multiple levels of representation more easily. Note that overbar is not a
function: f and $\overline{f}$ are merely distinct lexical symbols whose meanings are related.

some detail. Boyer and Moore used partial evaluation in a theorem prover for LISP functions [BM75], and Darlington and Burstall used it to optimise procedures [DB75]. So far, partial evaluators have not been sufficiently powerful to be widely useful, even though a team at Linköping University considered using partial evaluation as a general purpose programming tool as early as 1976 [BHOS76]. More recently, interest in partial evaluation has resurfaced as the process has become better understood.

In this section we will consider some of the most promising applications of program specialisation. Many of these have appeared in [Ersh82], [Fut83] and [Tur86] amongst others.

1.2.1   Automatic Compilation

Historically, automatic compilation was one of the earliest applications of partial evaluation to be proposed. Suppose that int is an interpreter for some language, and that $prog$ is a program in that language. When we run the program $prog$ using the interpreter along with some input data $data$ we compute the result,

$$result = int\ prog\ data$$

For many runs of int we would expect the $prog$ argument to be constant, varying only the $data$ argument. The same instructions will have to be interpreted again and again. Let us therefore specialise the interpreter to its first argument.

$$\overline{int_{prog}} = mix\ \overline{int}\ \overline{prog}$$

The result of the specialisation is a program (in the language in which $\overline{int}$ is *written*) which computes some function int_{prog}. By the correctness condition we know that,

$$int_{prog}\ data = int\ prog\ data$$

The action of int_{prog} on the data is the same as the action of $prog$ when interpreted by int. But, unlike $prog$, the function int_{prog} does not require an interpreter. Thus int_{prog} is a compiled equivalent of $prog$. The computations usually performed by int every time it is run will have been performed by mix during specialisation. These are the computations that relate to the static properties of $prog$. In principle, the only computations of *int* that int_{prog} needs to perform are those that depend on *data* (that is, on the dynamic properties of *prog*). Of course this is an idealistic picture. How far this ideal is attained depends on many factors.

This use of partial evaluation is known as the *first Futamura projection*.

1.2.2   Producing Compilers Automatically

We can take the process further. If we had many different programs to compile, we would compute $mix\ \overline{int}\ \overline{prog_i}$ for each of the programs $prog_i$. The $\overline{int}$ parameter to *mix* is unchanged in each of these computations. So it likewise makes sense to specialise *mix* to the interpreter program $\overline{int}$. How do we do this? We use *mix* itself. Applying the *mix* equation to itself gives

$$\overline{mix_{\overline{int}}} = mix\ \overline{mix}\ \overline{\overline{int}}$$

Again the result is a program computing a function. What sort of function is $mix_{\overline{int}}$? By the correctness condition,

$$
\begin{aligned}
mix_{\overline{int}}\ \overline{prog} &= mix\ \overline{int}\ \overline{prog} \\
&= \overline{int_{prog}}
\end{aligned}
$$

But $\overline{int_{prog}}$ is the compiled version of *prog*. The function $mix_{\overline{int}}$ is therefore playing the role of a compiler. This is the *second Futamura projection*. By specialising *mix* to an interpreter for some language we obtain a compiler for that language. There is, of course, no requirement that the two *mix*'s are identical as long as they are both specialisers, but there is a certain elegance when they are the same.

We can take one final step. If we have many interpreters to turn into compilers, we will need to calculate $mix\ \overline{mix}\ \overline{int_i}$ for each interpreter int_i. In each case the $\overline{mix}$ parameter remains unchanged. It makes sense, therefore, to specialise *mix* to itself.

$$\overline{mix_{\overline{mix}}} = mix\ \overline{mix}\ \overline{\overline{mix}}$$

By the correctness condition,

$$
\begin{aligned}
mix_{\overline{mix}}\ \overline{\overline{int}} &= mix\ \overline{mix}\ \overline{\overline{int}} \\
&= \overline{mix_{\overline{int}}}
\end{aligned}
$$

The function $mix_{\overline{mix}}$ is a compiler generator. Given an interpretive definition of a language (an executable denotational semantics, for example) $mix_{\overline{mix}}$ produces a compiler. The potential of this, the *third Futamura projection*, was actually first noticed by Turchin in 1979 [Tur79], but it was not until the mid-1980's that it was realised in practice. Working in a purely functional subset of LISP, the group at DIKU, Copenhagen, led by Neil Jones, produced a version of *mix* that was able to specialise a copy of itself to itself [JSS85]. Using the result (now called *cogen* by the Danish group) they were able to convert interpreters into compilers for a number of small example languages. The compilers produced code that ran between 5 and 20 times faster than the interpreted programs did, and the code quality of the compiler itself was quite reasonable. In Chapter 2 we will study their algorithms in some detail.

Understanding precisely the link between compilers and interpreters is important. Barzdin extracts a *compiler basis* from an interpreter and uses this to construct a compiler [Bar88]. Bulyonkov and Ershov have undertaken complementary work [BE88]. They attempt to understand where the traditional compiler structures come from. Where in an interpreter are the proto versions of object code templates, symbol tables, the stack, and so on? Is it possible for these structures to be created by partial evaluation alone?

1.2.3 Embedded Languages

The goal of producing compilers automatically for production languages is still some way off. Automatically generated compilers are unable to compete effectively against hand written compilers, and for commercially available languages it is worth expending human effort to obtain high quality. In other situations, automatically produced compilers are more appropriate. For example, Emanuelson and Haraldsson used partial evaluation to compile extensions to LISP [EH80]. The extensions were defined interpretively and, prior to execution, were optimised by partial evaluation. In the reference they give a detailed example involving a pattern matching extension. Their results compared well with those given by a commercial compiler.

The concept of language extension can be taken further. Some hard problems become more tractable through the use of an intermediate language. The programmer writes an interpreter for some problem-specific language, and then writes the solution to the problem in that language. Occasionally it is convenient to have more than one intermediate language and to form an interpretive tower, where each language interprets the one above. It is imperative to have some means of collapsing such towers automatically once the program is written, because each interpretive layer represents an order of magnitude loss of efficiency. Only when this is possible will this approach to programming become practicable.

So far, the applications have been orientated towards programming languages. There are other areas for which partial evaluation shows promise.

1.2.4 Ray Tracing

In his Master's thesis, Mogensen reports on an experiment involving ray tracing [Mog86]. A ray-tracer is a function *ray* of two arguments: a scene *s* and a viewpoint *v*. The result of computing *ray s v* is a picture of the scene as it appears from the given viewpoint. Typically, ray-tracers are heavily interpretive—many flow-of-control decisions are based on the scene which has to be constantly re-examined. If the the ray-tracer is specialised to the scene, these control decisions become built into the structure of the residual program. This program computes a function ray_s which, when given a viewpoint, draws the scene from that point. Because ray_s is no longer interpretive, the specialised ray-tracer is able to draw the scene rapidly from any required viewpoint.

Surprisingly, Mogensen found that even if only one view was required, it proved to be faster to specialise the ray-tracer and then run the specialised version, than it was to run the original. In retrospect the reason is clear. In the original ray-tracer the scene description is examined many times involving many repeated computations whereas in the specialised version these are reflected in the program structure. This parallels the familiar situation in programming where, for most programs, compiling then running the program is faster than using an interpreter.

Similar principles may be seen at work in the following (speculative) examples.

1.2.5 Theorem Proving

A theorem prover takes a set of axioms and a theorem, and determines whether the theorem is a consequence of the axioms or not. We could represent it as a function *prove* taking two arguments, axioms *a* and theorem *t*. Because of the interpretive nature of *prove* and because the set of axioms *a* may be used repeatedly, it makes sense to specialise *prove* to *a*. The result, $prove_a$, is a theorem prover optimised to prove theorems derivable from the axioms *a*. In essence *prove* is an interpreter for a restricted "programming language" where sets of axioms correspond to "programs". Rather than interpret the "program" *a* afresh for each new theorem, we "compile" *a* to give $prove_a$ to use instead.

Of course, instead of calculating $mix \ \overline{prove} \ \overline{a}$ directly, we can first use $mix_{\overline{mix}}$ to obtain a "compiler" for *prove*, namely $mix_{p\overline{rove}}$. We can use this and compute $mix_{p\overline{rove}} \ a$ to obtain $prove_a$. Moreover, if we have an alternate set of axioms a', we can apply $mix_{p\overline{rove}}$ to a' to produce $prove_{a'}$. This example shows that $mix_{\overline{mix}}$ is a compiler generator in a broad sense of the term and is not restricted to programming languages.

1.2.6   Expert Systems

Very similar methods may be applied to expert systems. We can regard an expert system as consisting of three parts, an inference engine *infer*, a set of rules *r* and a set of facts *f*. Let us suppose that the result, given by *infer r f*, is the set of facts deducible from *f* using the rules *r*. A general inference engine proceeds interpretively. It takes the set of facts, chooses a rule, and determines whether the rule is applicable to the facts. If so the newly inferred fact is added to the body of facts. Then the next rule is considered, and so on. In practice this approach turns out to be too slow to be useful, especially when many rules and facts are being manipulated. It is particularly acute when the expert system is hierarchical, i.e. when there are rules that govern the applicability of other rules. Usually, the problem is overcome by compiling the expert system by hand (a process which is tedious, error-prone, and time-consuming) yet the same effect may be obtained by specialisation. The residual program $infer_r$ is an inference engine customised to the set of rules *r*. It is a function from facts to facts that contains little or none of the original interpretive machinery. Of course, we cannot hope that the efficiency gained by automatic specialisation will be as great as is obtainable by hand, but the difference between the two may be quite small.

Turchin goes one stage further [Tur86]. Suppose that the body of rules is gradually increasing. We produce specialised versions of *infer* to perform inference according to the rules we already have, but we also retain the original unspecialised version of *infer* in case any new rules are added. This allows the expert system to grow. What is more, in quiet periods the inference engine could be specialised to the new set of rules to allow these to be handled more efficiently. This, Turchin postulates, may correspond with what happens to us during sleep.

Of course, rather than use the general specialiser again and again we would use $mix_{\overline{mix}}$ to produce one optimised to the task of specialising the inference engine *infer*. This is another example of "compiler generation".

These examples do not exhaust the possible applications for partial evaluation. As a final example, Consel and Danvy reported taking a clear but inefficient string matching algorithm and, by specialising it to the pattern, automatically produced what was essentially the Knuth-Morris-Pratt algorithm [CD89]. It is reasonable to expect that as partial evaluators become more powerful and robust many more applications will be found.

1.3   How Strong is a Partial Evaluator?

The equations given earlier actually say nothing about how efficient the programs resulting from partial evaluation are. The equations are consequences of the S-m-n theorem of recursive function theory. The theorem states that a specialised version of a recursive function is itself an effectively constructible recursive function (that is, there exists a recursive function which acts as a general specialiser). A direct implementation of the proof of the theorem leads to a trivial implementation of specialisation. Thus, suppose that $f\ x\ y$ is a two parameter function and that we wish to produce f_X using some value X for x. We can do so by defining

$$f_X\ y\ =\ f\ X\ y$$

and gain no improvement at all.

Fortunately, there are non-trivial implementations of partial evaluation but each differs in power. Jones suggests a test for assessing their strength. Suppose that s_int is a self interpreter for the language in which mix is written, so for any program $\overline{f}$,

$$s\_int\ \overline{f} = f$$

Then we would hope that

$$mix\ \overline{s\_int}\ \overline{\overline{f}}\ \simeq\ \overline{f}$$

where $\simeq$ is meant to imply that the two sides are comparable in size and efficiency. If this equation is satisfied then *mix* is able to remove a complete layer of interpretation.

1.4   Related Topics

As with every area of study, partial evaluation does not stand on its own. We have already alluded to the fact that it has much in common with compilation. One could argue that constant folding is like partial evaluation but on a very limited scale, and that function or procedure unfolding to produce in-line code is more so. Compiler generation techniques come even closer to *mix* technology. There has been active research in this area for some time producing familiar products like LEX and YACC. Another example is the Cornell Synthesizer Generator [RT89] which produces structure editors from grammars.

One motivation for automatic compiler generation is the difficulty of producing se-mantically correct, hand-written compilers. An automatic compiler generator would take a denotational (or other) description of some language and produce a compiler for that language. Any compiler generator needs to be proved correct, of course, but the proof only has to be done once. In contrast, *every* hand-produced compiler needs its own proof of correctness. An early attempt along these lines was Mosses' *semantics implementation system* [Mos79] but the residual programs produced by the system generally contained a large interpretive element. A later example, the CERES project [Tof84], produced better results through the use of more sophisticated techniques.

Schmidt has explored the possibility of automatically recognising which parameters in a denotational semantics may be implemented using the state or a stack etc. [Sch88], whereas Nielson uses a two level type system to separate compile-time and run-time computations [Nie88]. To attack the problem from a different direction, action se-mantics [MW87] defines interpreters in terms of combinators which manipulate *facets*. There are facets to capture variable binding, value manipulation, state transition and parallel communication. Facets are orthogonal in the sense that action in one facet is independent of action in the others. It is hoped that separating these facets may assist the production of efficient compilers.

There are also similarities between partial evaluation and more general program trans-formation methods. For example, fold/unfold transformations [BD77] are closely mimicked in specialisation. Methods of program analysis are also relevant. As we shall see in the next chapter, a prior program analysis is a vital part of the partial evaluation process. In Chapter 3 we explore the link between this *binding-time analysis* and the more familiar strictness analysis [AH87].

Turchin's *supercompilation* [Tur86] is more general than partial evaluation. The supercompiler *super*vises the evaluation of a program and *compiles* a residual program from it. Optimisation can occur even when no input data is present, through the use of *driving*. Expressions are driven across case-expressions, generating the information that (by assumption) the pattern succeeded. This information is used allowing for more reduction than by partial evaluation alone. The same principle is seen in Wadler's *deforestation* algorithm [Wad88]. Ensuring termination is still a big problem in partial evaluation, but it seems even worse when driving is present. Wadler addresses this issue by placing heavy restrictions on the form of function definitions to which his algorithm is applied. In contrast, Turchin applies his supercompiler to arbitrary programs and unites two states when they are "dangerously similar". This works in many cases though non-termination still occurs.

A similar extension to the standard techniques of partial evaluation may be achieved by using a theorem prover to propagate information from conditionals down each of the branches. This *generalised partial computation* [FN88] manipulates predicates as "static values", and these may allow more reduction to be performed than would otherwise be the case.

1.5 Mix Curries Programs

Before we close this chapter it will be useful to consider the types of objects given to and returned by *mix*. Its arguments are two pieces of program, the first representing a function of two arguments, and the second representing a value suitable for the function's first argument. Let us write $\overline{T}$ for the type of program code representing an object of type T. Thus, using the previous notation, if $t \in T$ then $\overline{t} \in \overline{T}$. Then,

$$mix : \overline{A \times B \to C} \times \overline{A} \ \to \ \overline{B \to C}$$

That is, *mix* takes a definition of a two argument function and a definition of a value for the first argument, and produces a definition of the corresponding function of the remaining argument.

What is the type of $mix_{\overline{mix}}$? Substituting into the type definition of mix gives,

$$mix_{\overline{mix}} : \overline{\overline{A \times B \to C}} \;\to\; \overline{A} \;\to\; \overline{B \to C}$$

Given a definition of a program specifying a two argument function $mix_{\overline{mix}}$ returns a program which, when executed, takes a definition of a value, and returns a program to compute the corresponding function of the remaining argument.

These equations motivate the slogan: *partial evaluation is Currying on programs*[2].

---

[2]Note that although we have used the Curried notation at various points in the chapter, evaluation normally requires all arguments to be present before any reduction can take place. Thus, as far as standard evaluation is concerned, Curried functions are actually little different from their un-Curried cousins.

Chapter 2

Partial Evaluation in Practice

Having seen some of the principles of partial evaluation we now consider practicalities. In this chapter we will study the standard algorithm used in partial evaluation and introduce an extended example which we develop throughout the thesis. The material of this chapter draws very heavily on the experience of the DIKU group and much of the material presented here may be found in [JSS85], [Ses86] and [JSS89].

Partial evaluation has been attempted in a number of different programming paradigms. The earliest work used LISP-like languages because programs in such languages can easily be treated as data. In particular, the first self-applicable partial evaluator was written in a purely functional subset of first-order, statically scoped LISP. Since then work has been done to incorporate other language features of LISP-like languages including, for example, global variables [BD89]. A self-applicable partial evaluator for a term rewriting language has been achieved [Bon89], and more recently a higher-order λ-calculus version has been developed [Gom89].

Because of these successes, partial evaluation is sometimes linked with functional languages. Indeed the word "evaluation" itself is expression orientated. However, partial evaluation has also become popular in logic languages, and in Prolog in particular. Kursawe, investigating "pure partial evaluation", shows that the principles are the same in both the logic and functional paradigms [Kur88]. Using the referentially opaque `clause` primitive, very compact interpreters (and hence partial evaluators) can be written. However, it is not clear how the `clause` predicate itself should be handled by a partial evaluator and, hence, whether this approach can ever lead to self-application. Other "features" of Prolog that can cause problems for partial evaluation are the cut and negation-by-failure. Lloyd and Shepherson have addressed

13

some of these [LS87]. However, by restricting themselves to the clean parts of Prolog, Fuller and Abramsky have achieved a self-applicable partial evaluator [FA88]. Their method is directly equivalent to the functional approach used at DIKU.

Every language paradigm introduces its own problems, and this is also true in the imperative case. The early LISP work, for example, concentrated only on functional aspects because the imperative features seemed too difficult. Surprisingly, however, a fully self-applicable partial evaluator for a small imperative language has been reported [GJ89]. The language consists of a sequence of commands, which are assignment, conditionals, or `goto`s. Values are S-expressions manipulated using the standard LISP primitives. A few other operators are provided. Not only are the resulting compilers reasonably small and efficient, but they also exhibit much of the structure of hand-written compilers.

Much of the interest in partial evaluation in the Soviet Union focuses on imperative languages and on Pascal in particular. There the process is called *polyvariant mixed computation* [Bul88]. Technically, *mixed computation* is more general than partial evaluation. It includes any semantics preserving process that operates on a mix of program and data. The adjective *polyvariant* describes the situation where one program fragment may be specialised to many different states thereby producing more than one descendent fragment in the residual program. We will see this idea in the functional model. In the Soviet work, the state is split into two parts—the *accessible* and the *inaccessible*. As one might expect this is equivalent to the static/dynamic separation. Analysis is harder in the imperative case because both procedural unfolding and evaluation of expressions may sometimes be invalid. Nonetheless, results have been interesting: for example, Ostrovsky uses mixed computation as part of the process of producing industrial quality parsers [Ost88].

It is interesting to note that all the self-applicable partial evaluators reported to date use S-expressions as their sole data structure. This situation must change if partial evaluation is to gain a place as an everyday programming tool. We will return to this point at the end of the thesis.

2.1 The Partial Evaluation Process

We will present the specialisation algorithm using a functional language. The DIKU group implemented *mix* in a subset of purely functional statically scoped LISP but for consistency with the rest of the thesis we will use a typed lazy functional language.

There are two stages to specialisation. The pre-processing phase takes a program and information about what data will be present initially, and returns an annotated program. From this annotated program and the partial data the second phase produces the residual program. In most cases, the two phases could be performed together with only a small loss of efficiency. For self-application, however, it turns out to be crucial to separate the phases. If this is not done, the generated programs (compilers etc.) are huge and inefficient. The reason for this is discussed in Section 2.2.

The first phase itself consists of two interdependent parts. These are called *binding-time analysis* (or BTA for short), and *call annotation*. Binding-time analysis determines which expressions will be evaluated during partial evaluation, and call annotation decides which function calls will be unfolded. The result of this phase is an annotated program. If $\overline{prog}$ is the original program then we write $\overline{prog}^{ann}$ for the annotated version.

2.1.1 Binding-Time Analysis

The purpose of binding-time analysis is to discover which expressions within the program can be evaluated by the partial evaluator given the limited amount of data that will be present. The analysis can be performed by abstract interpretation. In this chapter we follow the DIKU work and treat values atomically. That is, if an expression contains any dynamic part, then we will consider the whole expression to be dynamic.

The abstract domain of values is the two point domain $\{S, D\}$ where $S \sqsubseteq D$. To associate S with an expression indicates that the expression is totally static—it can be fully evaluated during partial evaluation. In contrast, D indicates that the expression may be dynamic, i.e. it is not possible to guarantee that it can be evaluated during partial evaluation.

As ever, the analysis is approximate in that there may be some expressions that are classified as dynamic which could actually be evaluated. The converse never applies: an expression is only classified as static if it can definitely be evaluated. The result of the binding-time analysis is an annotated program where the parameters of each function are either classified as static or as dynamic.

2.1.2   Call annotation

A partial evaluator that never unfolded function calls could make little improvement to the programs to which it was applied. Conversely, if a partial evaluator unfolded all function calls, it would be unlikely to terminate. We must decide, therefore, which function calls to unfold and which to leave folded. Rather than classify the functions themselves as unfoldable or non-unfoldable, we annotate individual function calls. So a particular function may be unfolded in one place but not in another. Function calls to be unfolded are called *eliminable*, those that are to remain are called *residual*.

In the early *mix* work call annotations were inserted by hand. Subsequently, Sestoft described an analysis, called *call graph analysis*, which can deduce the annotations automatically [Ses88]. The analysis takes a program having static/dynamic annotations and inserts call annotations. But, because a residual call cannot be unfolded, its result cannot be classified as static, so call annotations might cause some expressions, previously considered static, to become dynamic. Thus, after call annotation, the program must have its static/dynamic annotations recomputed. The new annotations may in turn force some calls, previously considered eliminable, to become residual, and so on.

Fortunately this process is monotonic—no dynamic annotation ever becomes static and no residual call ever becomes eliminable. Termination of the process is therefore ensured. In practice, the cycle is rarely followed more than a couple of times before a limit is found.

To summarise: the annotations resulting from the first phase of the partial evaluation process classify parameters as static or dynamic and function calls as residual or eliminable. Primitive operators may also be annotated. If all their arguments are present they are eliminable, otherwise they are residual. Once annotated, the program is ready to be specialised.

2.1.3   Specialisation

Imagine we have a function f defined by $f\ x\ y = e$ where x is static and y dynamic. Further suppose that we wish to specialise f to a value a for x. We evaluate e in an environment in which x is bound to a. As the environment binds static values only, the result of the evaluation is an expression which, in this case, may involve y.

Depending on the annotations in e, some function calls may remain in the residual expression. Suppose, for example, there is a residual call to f with a value a' for its x parameter. We wish to replace this call also with a call to a specialised version of f, this time specialised to the value a'. Producing this new specialised version may, in turn, generate new function/argument pairs that also need to be replaced with specialised versions, and so on. This process continues until all residual function calls are replaced with calls to appropriate specialised functions. This is the functional counterpart of polyvariant specialisation.

We can describe the algorithm more generally. We are given a list of function names paired with values for their static parameters. This is called the *pending* list, and identifies which functions need to be specialised to which values. There is also a list of function/value pairs for which specialised versions have already been produced. We repeatedly select and remove an element from the *pending* list. If the appropriate specialised version has already been produced, we go on to the next one. Otherwise, we obtain the relevant function definition from the program, giving the static and dynamic parameters along with the function body. The function body is evaluated in the partial environment (binding the static names to the static values) resulting in a residual expression which forms the body of the new specialised function. The new body is scanned to find any function calls that may require specialisation and these are appended to the *pending* list. An implementation of the algorithm in LML appears in Appendix C.

The result of specialisation is a list of new function definitions. Initially the new residual functions are named by the original function name together with the values of the static parameters. Later on, a new function name is generated for each such pair, and the program consistently renamed. During renaming, the static parameters disappear completely from the program. The specialised functions retain their dynamic parameters only.

2.1.4 Two Small Examples

It is worth looking at some small examples. These emphasise the point made in Chapter 1 that partial evaluation has more applications than just language interpreters and compilers. The first is the standard exponentiation function.

```
power n x = if    n=0
```

```
then   1
else   x * power (n-1) x
```

We will specialise power's first argument to the value 3. The first parameter is static and the second dynamic. This is consistent with the recursive call, for if the value of n can be computed, then so can the corresponding value (n-1) in the recursive call. The specialised function will lose the static parameter and be a function of the dynamic parameter x only. In this example the recursive call may be safely unfolded so it is classified as eliminable.

Evaluating the body of the function in the environment in which n is bound to 3 gives the residual expression x * (x * (x * 1)). All the conditionals have been reduced and the recursive calls unfolded. The (re-named) residual function is, therefore,

```
power_3 x = x * (x * (x * 1))
```

(Note that simplifying (x * 1) to x requires the laws of arithmetic, not just partial evaluation). This residual function is more efficient than the original. Instead of having to evaluate a series of conditionals and perform a number of function calls the calculation is performed directly.

The previous example shows only some aspects of partial evaluation. A richer example is given by Ackerman's function.

```
ack m n = if     m=0
          then   n+1
          else   if     n=0
                 then   ack (m-1) 1
                 else   ack (m-1) (ack m (n-1))
```

Suppose we intend to specialise ack to the value 2 for its first parameter m. As before the first parameter can be classified as static and the second as dynamic. However, in this case the final two recursive calls should not be unfolded and must be classified as residual, but as the first recursive call (ack (m-1) 1) has static information for all its parameters it can be unfolded.

Initially the pending list contains only the pair (ack, [2]). There is only one static parameter to ack so the list of static values has only one element. The new body, produced by partial evaluation, is the expression

```
if    n=0
then  3
else  ack 1 (ack 2 (n-1))
```

The outer conditional has been reduced but the inner one remains because it depends on a dynamic value. The two recursive calls are present as they were annotated as residual, and so when this expression is scanned for residual calls the list [(ack,[1]), (ack,[2])] is produced. This is appended onto the end of the (now empty) pending list for the recursive call of the specialiser.

Next, a version of ack specialised to the static value 1 is produced in exactly the same way. Then, in the following recursive call to the specialiser, the pending list has the value [(ack,[2]), (ack, [0]), (ack, [1])]. Because a version of ack specialised to [2] has already been produced, the first of these is discarded and ack is specialised to [0]. After this process has been repeated a couple of times the pending list will be empty and the process will terminate. After renaming, the result will be the program

```
ack_0 n = n+1

ack_1 n = if    n=0
            then  2
            else  ack_0 (ack_1 (n-1))

ack_2 n = if    n=0
            then  3
            else  ack_1 (ack_2 (n-1))
```

With only half the number of conditionals per function call, the residual program is noticeably more efficient than the original. There is a price to pay, however. It is also larger that the original. While there is, in principle, no limit to the increase in size the DIKU group found that a linear growth (with respect to the sum of the sizes of program and data) is typical of most examples.

In each of these examples the gain in efficiency is around 300%. This is fairly low for partial evaluation as, in each case, the original programs contained only a moderate interpretive element. At the end of this chapter we will introduce a larger example that will be developed throughout the thesis. This will have a more significant interpretive element and so larger gains can be expected.

2.2   Self-Application

We recall from Chapter 1 that self-application of a partial evaluator is required in order to produce compilers and compiler generators. The first attempts at self-application created huge residual programs. On examination it turned out that *mix* was not obtaining sufficient information to perform reductions on the partial evaluator appearing in its first argument. To make this clear imagine that we are computing

$$\overline{mix_{int}} = mix_1 \; \overline{mix_2} \; \overline{\overline{int}}$$

(We number the two occurrences of *mix* to distinguish between them in the explanation—otherwise the two are identical). The program $\overline{mix}$ contains an evaluator which reduces static expressions. Any static expressions in $\overline{mix_2}$ can be recognised during partial evaluation even without binding-time analysis, and can be reduced accordingly (using the evaluator in $\overline{mix_1}$). However, the decision whether or not to apply the evaluator in $\overline{mix_2}$ to expressions in $\overline{int}$ depends on which parts of the input to $\overline{int}$ are to be static when the compiler $mix_{\overline{int}}$ is used. Without binding-time annotations, this information is dynamic. This means that very little reduction can be performed, resulting in bulky and inefficient compilers.

The insight that allowed the DIKU group to circumvent this problem is that it is sufficient to know which expressions of $\overline{int}$ are static or dynamic. The actual values are not required. Thus, if $\overline{int}$ is annotated appropriately by a preprocessing phase, then mix_1 is able to decide when to apply the evaluator appearing in $\overline{mix_2}$. The *mix* equation should, therefore, be expressed as

$$\overline{int_{prog}} = mix \; \overline{int}^{ann} \; \overline{prog}$$

so that when self-application takes place we get

$$\overline{mix_{\overline{int}}} = mix_1 \; \overline{mix_2}^{ann} \; \overline{int}^{ann}$$

The annotations on $\overline{int}$ are available for $\overline{mix_2}$ and allow its evaluator to be applied. It is the annotations on *mix*'s *second* argument, therefore, that allows efficient compilers to be produced.

This insight defines what is essentially a new binding-time. We are already familiar with static and dynamic binding-times. A static value will be present during partial evaluation, whereas dynamic values are not available until run-time. In order to allow self-application there must be some information that is even more static than the static values. It must not depend on the static values themselves, but only on the knowledge that there will, at partial evaluation time, be such static values. This sort of information is called *metastatic* [Mog89]. Binding-time analysis must be metastatic. If it is not (that is, if the analysis ever uses the actual static values), then the results will be of no use in self-application.

2.3   Congruence and Finiteness

There are other constraints that binding-time analysis must satisfy. Not only must the analysis be metastatic, but the resulting annotations must be *congruent* and *finite*. We will study congruence in some detail in Chapter 3 but for now we will confine ourselves to informal definitions and intuitions.

Stated simply, *congruence* requires that static values only ever depend on static values and never on dynamic values. For example, suppose we have the following function definition.

```
f x y = if   x=0
        then y
        else f (x-1) (x*y)
```

If f's first parameter is dynamic then its second must also be dynamic. This is because the value of f's second parameter in the recursive call depends on the (dynamic) value of its first. As we noted before, the aim of specialisation is to omit static parameters in the residual program. If we make y static while x is dynamic, and we specialise f to the value 2 (for y) then we have a problem. Which specialised version of f should be used to replace the recursive call? The answer is that there is no single call that is sufficient. Instead we have to replace it with an infinitely branching conditional giving a residual function of the form

```
f_2 x = if   x=0
```

```
              then  2
              else  case x in
                        1 -> f_2 (x-1)
                        2 -> f_4 (x-1)
                              :
```

This is clearly undesirable! However, if the result of binding-time analysis is congruent, then it is always possible to calculate the static parameters of each function call during partial evaluation. As a result, there is a single residual function with which to replace each original call. Furthermore, the only conditionals to appear in the residual program originate from the source program—none need to be added. The residual program is, in this sense, "congruent" with the source program.

In addition to congruence, the results of binding-time analysis must be *finite*. As congruent annotations produce a congruent program, so finite annotations lead to a finite residual program. Consider the following example.

```
    f x y = if    y=0
             then  x
             else  f (x+1) (y-1)
```

We declare x to be static and y dynamic. This is congruent but not finite. Suppose we specialise f to the value 1 for x. Making the recursive call residual, we obtain the following residual program.

```
    f_1 y = if    y=0
             then  1
             else  f_2 (y-1)

    f_2 y = if    y=0
             then  2
             else  f_3 (y-1)

    . . .  etc.
```

Annotating the recursive call as eliminable does not help. While we would then have only a single residual function, its body would be infinite in size. Poor call annotations can in themselves cause infinite unfolding, but good call annotations cannot cause an inherently infinite annotation to become finite.

Jones describes an analysis using a three point domain that goes some way to producing a finite annotation [Jon88]. The only time its results may not be finite is if the program contains an infinite loop. Under strict semantics the program would not terminate anyway, and so, it is argued, it is not unreasonable for the partial evaluation to loop also. Unfortunately, however, under non-strict semantics, exactly the same program may be very well behaved. Indeed infinite structures are a popular and powerful programming method in lazy languages. There is a need therefore for further work in this area. In the rest of the thesis we will sidestep this issue. The binding-time analysis given in Chapter 4 produces congruent annotations but they are not necessarily finite. How to achieve this in general is still an open problem.

In the remainder of this chapter we introduce the example which will be developed throughout the thesis.

2.4   Example

Our main example concerns automatic compilation. Using a fairly standard (first-order) lazy functional language notation, we define an interpreter for a block structured imperative language. Programs in this language are constructed from assignment, conditional, and while statements. New variables are introduced using the `Alloc` declaration and are in scope in the block immediately following. Blocks are sequences of statements, represented as lists. Communication with the outside world takes place via streams (lists). The `Read` command retrieves the first value from the input stream and the `Write` command places a value on the output stream. Commands may be represented as terms of the following datatype,

```
type Command =   Read Ident
               + Write Exp
               + Alloc Ident [Command]
               + DeAlloc
               + Assign Ident Exp
               + If Exp [Command] [Command]
               + While Exp [Command]
```

with appropriate definitions for the types Ident and Exp (we will consider integer expressions only and represent booleans as integers). The DeAlloc variant does not correspond with a command, but the interpreter uses it to mark the end of a variable's scope. Each of the others correspond directly with commands. The following is provided as an example of programs in this language. Its action is to find the maximum of a series of inputs (terminated by 0).

```
Alloc X
  [ Alloc Y
      [ Assign Y zero,
        Read X,
        While (greater (var X) zero)
          [ If (greater (var X) (var Y)) [Assign Y (var X)] [],
            Read X ],
        Write (var Y) ] ]
```

where zero, greater, and var are the obvious functions associated with the expression type Exp. Notice that the effect of an If without an else branch is achieved by supplying an empty list of commands as the else part.

The interpreter is inspired by continuation semantics, following about as closely as is possible in a first-order language. The main function **exec** takes a list of instructions and the input stream, and returns the output stream. It achieves this by calling the function **run**, starting it off with an empty state which will contain the variables and their values when augmented by any Alloc statements. Because of a deficiency of the binding-time analysis we are considering at the moment, the state is split into two parts: a name list and a value list. This allows the names to be static while the values are dynamic. Once the interpreter reaches the end of the program the output stream is terminated. The definitions are,

```
exec block inp = run block [] [] inp

run    []        ns vs inp = []
run (com:coms) ns vs inp
  = case com in
        Read k
          -> run coms ns (update ns vs k (hd inp)) (tl inp)
```

```
Write e
   -> eval ns vs e : run coms ns vs inp
Alloc k cs
   -> run (cs++(DeAlloc:coms)) (k:ns) (0:vs) inp
DeAlloc
   -> run coms (tl ns) (tl vs) inp
Assign k e
   -> run coms ns (update ns vs k (eval ns vs e)) inp
If e cs1 cs2
   -> if    (eval ns vs e = 0)
      then  (run (cs2++coms) ns vs inp)
      else  (run (cs1++coms) ns vs inp)
While e cs
   -> run [If e (cs++(com:coms)) coms] ns vs inp
```

There are two non-standard aspects to this definition. Firstly, in the interpretation, the block structure is flattened and implemented explicitly (using DeAlloc) rather than by using recursion to do so implicitly. Secondly, looping is performed by appending the body of the loop to the front of the program. The implementation makes use of the law that states that ⟦while E C⟧ has the same behaviour as ⟦if E then (C;While E C)⟧. We will leave a discussion of the motivation for these choices until the conclusion.

The auxiliary functions referred to by run have fairly standard definitions. The expression evaluator eval uses the state to supply values for variables. It cannot cause side effects on the state but just returns an integer result. In contrast, update returns a new value list in which the value associated with the named variable is replaced with the new value.

If, in the initial call, the block input to exec is supplied but the input stream inp is not, then significant gains can be achieved by partial evaluation. The first two parameters to run are static, the other two dynamic. This means that residual versions of run have only the value list and the input list as parameters. In order to ensure finite unfolding the call to run in the While case should be made residual. Everywhere else the program parameter decreases in size, so finiteness is guaranteed. Calls to the update function (and its sibling lookup which will appear in eval) must all be made residual. These functions will have versions specialised to each of the variables that they are used with.

To see what the results are like we will specialise **exec** to the example program above.
There is a single **While** loop so only one residual version of **run** is produced.

```
exec inp
  = run (update_x (update_y [0,0] 0) (hd inp)) (tl inp)


run vs inp
  = if    lookup_x vs > 0
    then  if    lookup_x vs > lookup_y vs
          then  run (update_x (update_y vs (lookup_x vs))
                              (hd inp))
                    (tl inp)
          else  run (update_x vs (hd inp)) (tl inp)
    else  lookup_y vs : []
```

The residual versions of **update** and **lookup** will be fairly efficient. For example,

```
update_x n (v1:v2:vs) = v1 : n : vs
update_y n (v1:vs)    = n : vs
```

There are no comparisons of variable names in order to find the correct place in the
value list. Those actions are performed during partial evaluation.

The residual interpreter (which is a compiled version of the input program) is far
more efficient than the original interpreted version. It is not as good as a hand
written program for finding the maximum in a list, but is not a long way off. As a
program produced by automatic compilation the results are satisfactory.

Some problems remain however. The first concerns the call annotations. In the
interpreter code handling an **If** statement, the same code suffix **coms** appears in
both branches of the if...then...else... expression. This means that some code
duplication may take place in the residual program. An example appears above in
the body of the residual version of **run**. Looking at the the inner conditional, we
see that the expression (update_x ... (hd inp)) occurs in both branches. Both
occurrences arise from a single occurrence of **Read x** in the input program. It so
happens that in this example, this is actually desirable, but for input programs with
nested conditionals the growth in residual program size could be quite disastrous.

The solution to this problem is to make each of the recursive calls to run residual. This produces a less pleasing result in some ways, but prevents any possible code explosion. In most cases each instruction in the input program leads to a single residual function. The exceptions are Alloc and While, which each lead to two versions. Thus, the size of the residual program will be linear in the size of the input program. Many of these function calls may be unfolded in a post-processing phase. Jones calls this *transition compression* [Jon88].

A second problem concerns the residual versions of update and lookup. Because the residual state is represented as a list, these perform a great deal of heap manipulation with associated time penalties. All that they are actually doing is accessing or replacing values in a fixed length list. Even more serious, however, is the third problem. In order to obtain any worthwhile results whatsoever, we were forced to separate the state into two components, the name list and the value list, even though the most natural structure is a list of pairs. This flies in the face of one of the aims of partial evaluation, namely, to allow increased modularity. It is these last two issues that are addressed in the ensuing chapters.

Chapter 3

Static Projections

The equations for *mix* assume that it is operating on a two argument function where the first argument is static and the second dynamic. This is the canonical case. In practice we cannot hope that all functions will turn out this way. For example, a function may have many arguments, the first and third being static, say. Alternatively, a single argument may have both static and dynamic parts. We need a framework for reducing the general case to the canonical case.

We can simplify the general case by requiring that all functions have exactly one argument. In first-order languages this is no real restriction. Functions must always be applied to all their arguments, so we can just express them as a single tuple. The next stage is to factorise this single (composite) argument into two parts, the static and the dynamic. We use the results of binding-time analysis to control the factorisation.

Note that, even though functions will only have one argument, we will still loosely describe them as having many. For example, we will talk of a function `f (x,y) = ...` as having two arguments when this is appropriate.

3.1   Motivation

For the present we will focus our attention on the static part of the argument. To select the static part, we use a function from the argument domain to some domain of static values. If we make the static domain a sub-domain of the original we can simply "blank out" the dynamic part of the argument and leave the static part unchanged. We use $\bot$ to model the fact that nothing is known statically about dynamic data. Here $\bot$ has its fundamental meaning of "no information"—we get no static information from a dynamic value ($\bot$ is often associated with non-termination, but this is a secondary and derived interpretation. As a non-terminating computation gives no information about its result, $\bot$ is its natural value).

As an example, suppose that the original domain is $A \times B$ where B's value is static and A's dynamic. Then the function that selects the static part will be the map $(a, b) \mapsto (\bot, b)$. We can generalise this example to arbitrary domains by using *domain projections*.

Definition
A *projection* γ on a domain D is a continuous function $\gamma : D \to D$ such that (i) $\gamma \sqsubseteq ID$, and (ii) $\gamma \circ \gamma = \gamma$ (idempotence).

The first condition ensures that a projection adds no new information. This accords with the intuition that we can know no more about the static part of a value than we knew about the value originally. The second condition ensures that the function picks out the static part in one go. We will not need to repeatedly apply the function to check that the result we have really does represent the static part.

There are two important projections, *ID* and *ABS*, which crop up frequently. *ID* is the identity function—used when the argument is completely static—and *ABS* is the constant function that always returns $\bot$—used when the argument is completely dynamic.

In general we cannot hope to find a projection that selects *all* the static part of an argument, but we should guarantee that what is selected is actually static. This means that we will often make do with a projection that is smaller than ideal, for if a projection γ selects only static information from some argument then any projection smaller than γ does also (smaller in the usual function space ordering). As in Chapter 2, therefore, "static" means "definitely available during partial evaluation".

3.2   Other Uses of Projections

The projections we have defined are special cases of a more general class of functions called *retractions* (or *retracts* for short). Retractions are idempotent continuous functions, but need bear no relation to the identity function. Scott [Sco76] used *closures* (retractions greater than *ID*) to pick out sub-domains of $\mathbf{P}\omega$. The range of a closure is always a Scott domain, but this is not true for arbitrary retracts. The image of any projection is always a consistently complete, complete partial order, but is not necessarily algebraic. (Recall that a Scott domain is a complete partial order (so having a bottom element $\perp$, and limits of directed sets) which is also consistently complete (every set with an upper bound has a least upper bound) and ω-algebraic (every element is the limit of its finite approximations, there being only countably many finite elements)). Scott describes as *finitary* those projections whose image is algebraic, and hence a domain. All the projections used in this thesis are finitary.

Embedding/projection pairs (often just called projection pairs) crop up frequently in foundational issues in domain theory. They occur in the inverse limit construction, for example. An embedding/projection pair consists of two functions. One, the projection, maps from a larger domain to a smaller one and the other, the embedding, from the smaller to the larger. Applying the projection after the embedding gives the identity function, and applying the embedding after the projection gives a function weaker than the identity. A projection from a domain to itself corresponds to this latter composition. Projection pairs will be important to us in Chapter 5 where they are used in the dependent sum construction. However, most relevant to us for the present is the use of projections in strictness analysis.

3.2.1 Strictness Analysis

It is well known that the halting problem is uncomputable. That is, it is impossible to write a program that, given any input program, can *always* tell if it terminates or not. However, there are many programs which clearly do terminate, and there are many which clearly do not. This means that we can write an analysis program which approximates the halting problem in the following sense: if the analysis can be sure that the input program definitely loops then it will say so, otherwise it will suppose it halts. If we consider the answer HALTS to be greater than the answer LOOPS then we are approximating the halting problem from above—the algorithm will always give an answer at least as great as the true one. Strictness analysis is such an approximation. A function f is called *strict* if $f \perp = \perp$, so strictness analysis attempts to answer the question: if I give my function no information (typically, by applying it to a non-terminating computation) then does it also return no information?

Strictness analysis has provoked a lot of interest because of its use in improving the quality of compiled code from lazy functional languages. There are essentially two main approaches to the analysis, forwards and backwards. Forwards analysis ([AH87]) attempts to address the strictness question directly by considering if the function returns $\perp$ when applied to $\perp$. In contrast, backwards analysis considers how demand is propagated. It deduces how much input a function requires to produce a certain amount of output. The name "backwards analysis" arises because information is propagated from a function result to its argument. A detailed development may be found in [Hug88]. One way to specify "a certain amount" of information is to use domain projections [WH87]. From our point of view this is immediately promising. By having both strictness analysis and binding-time analysis cast in the same framework we may hope that the techniques of one will be applicable in the other. Indeed, we will see an example of this in Chapter 7.

Suppose, we are performing a backwards analysis and want to know how much of its argument some function $f : X \to Y$ needs in order to be able to return γ's worth of result (where γ is some projection $\gamma : Y \to Y$). Let us call this amount β (a projection $\beta : X \to X$). How are f, γ, and β related? The answer is that they must satisfy the *safety* condition:

$$\gamma \circ f = \gamma \circ f \circ \beta$$

Consider applying both sides to some value x. The safety condition implies that the application of $(\gamma \circ f)$ to x gives exactly the same value as applying it to $(\beta\ x)$. So to get γ's worth of information about the result of $(f\ x)$ we only need to know β's worth about x. Of course, we could still get at least γ's worth if we knew more about x. That is, if δ is another projection such that $\beta \sqsubseteq \delta$ then $\gamma \circ f = \gamma \circ f \circ \delta$ also holds. This means that it is always acceptable for a backwards strictness analyser to approximate upwards—a larger projection than the optimum will still be safe. In backwards analysis smaller projections convey more accurate information.

There is nothing about the safety condition that forces it to be used with backwards analysis. We can also interpret it in terms of forwards analysis. If I know β's worth about the argument to f then $\gamma \circ f = \gamma \circ f \circ \beta$ implies that I know at least γ's worth about the result of f. Further, for some projection δ where $\delta \sqsubseteq \gamma$ it is also true that $\delta \circ f = \delta \circ f \circ \beta$, so it is safe to approximate the result downwards. In forwards analysis larger projections convey more accurate information.

As the safety condition is applicable to both forward and backward analyses it is reasonable to ask which method is more suitable for a particular analysis problem. In binding-time analysis we start with an initial description of the input parameters and this information is propagated through the program. The direction of information flow is from argument to result, so we will use a forwards analysis.

There is an equivalent formulation of the safety condition that is often useful in proofs, namely, that $\gamma \circ f = \gamma \circ f \circ \beta$ holds exactly when $\gamma \circ f \sqsubseteq f \circ \beta$ holds. The proof follows easily from the fact that both γ and β are projections, and may be found in [WH87]. We will freely swap between the two formulations and use whichever is most appropriate at the time.

3.3   Congruence

Given a program and a description of which parts of the input are static, binding-time analysis produces a projection for each of the functions in the program. The analysis may only produce a projection γ for a function f if γ is a static projection for the argument of f wherever f is called. But, there may be a place in which the argument to f is given by the result of some other function, g say. We may know how much of the argument to g is static, but what do we mean when we say the result of g (and hence the argument to f) is static?

In [Jon88] Jones defines *congruence* to answer this question. Congruence has become the standard correctness condition in binding-time analysis for partial evaluation. We have already come across it informally, but in this chapter we give a precise definition. As we show, congruence is actually weaker than safety. However, it turns out that it is too weak to be suitable for most partial evaluators. A more suitable variant which, for the purpose of distinguishing the two, we call uniform congruence, is equivalent to the safety condition.

Jones models a program in terms of its stepwise behaviour and then uses this model to define congruence. The program is regarded as a triple (P, V, nx) where P is a set of program points, V a set of values (states) and nx a step function mapping (p, v) pairs into (p', v') pairs. Each (p, v) pair represents a single point in the computation, and the function nx defines a single computation step—from program point p and value v the computation proceeds to program point p' and value v'. The program is understood to have terminated with value v whenever $nx\ (p, v) = (p, v)$. In functional programs, the program points are the function names.

The choice of the destination program point under the action of nx depends, in general, on both the initial program point and the value. So from any given program point p, the destination point depends on the value at that point. At p, therefore, we can partition the value set V into subsets V_i such that if $v \in V_i$ then the destination point is p_i. Moreover, we can define functions $f_i : V_i \to V$ such that $v \in V_i \Rightarrow nx\ (p, v) = (p_i, f_i\ v)$. Such a choice of partition and functions is called a *control transfer*. A collection of control transfers, one for each program point, is called a *control structure*.

Congruence is defined in terms of a control structure and a program *division*. A division consists of three collections of functions—static, dynamic, and pairing functions—indexed by the program points. We will typically call these σ, δ, and π respectively, each duly subscripted with the program point. The purpose of the pairing function is to ensure that σ and δ are well-behaved with respect to each other through the requirement that $\pi_p \circ <\sigma_p, \delta_p> = ID$ (at each program point p). We give the precise definition of divisions in Chapter 5, but have sufficient for the present.

Definition (Jones)
A division (σ, δ, π) is *congruent* at a program point p with respect to a control structure $\{(V_i,\ f_i : V_i \to V)\}$ if for each i,

$$\forall v, w \in V_i\ .\ \sigma_p\ v = \sigma_p\ w \ \Rightarrow\ \sigma_{p_i}\ (f_i\ v) = \sigma_{p_i}\ (f_i\ w)$$

The definition requires that any two values with equal static parts are mapped to new values whose static parts are also equal. Thus, if a division is congruent we will be able, during partial evaluation, to calculate the static part of a value at any point in the computation: we can calculate the initial static value—it is given to us—and if we assume we can calculate the static value at some program point, congruence ensures that we will be able to calculate it at its immediate successors. Induction completes the proof. Congruence, therefore, satisfies the intuitive requirements we discussed in Chapter 2. Given a congruent division we can always calculate the value of $\sigma_p\ v$ and so can always choose which specialised version of p will replace (p, v).

3.4   Uniform Congruence

To justify the earlier claim that congruence is too weak a condition for most partial evaluators we will consider an example. Suppose we have the function,

```
p0 (x,y) = if    y=3
             then  p1 (x*y)
             else  p2 x
```

and a division where $\sigma_{p_0} = \mathit{fst}$, $\sigma_{p_1} = \mathit{ID}$ and $\sigma_{p_2} = \mathit{ID}$ where $\mathit{fst}\ (x, y) = x$. The set of values V at p_0 is $\mathbf{N} \times \mathbf{N}$ and the control structure is given by,

$$
\begin{aligned}
V_1 &= \{(x, 3) \mid x \in \mathbf{N}\} \\
V_2 &= \{(x, y) \mid x \in \mathbf{N}, y \in \mathbf{N} \setminus \{3\}\}
\end{aligned}
$$

The transfer functions are given by

$$
\begin{aligned}
f_1\ (x, y) &= x \times y \\
f_2\ (x, y) &= x
\end{aligned}
$$

To see that this division is congruent suppose that $v, w \in V_1$ and that $\sigma_{p_0}\ v = \sigma_{p_0}\ w$. Then

$$
\begin{aligned}
\sigma_{p_1}\ (f_1\ v) &= f_1\ v \\
&= \mathit{fst}\ v\ \times\ 3 \qquad [\text{definition of } f_1] \\
&= \mathit{fst}\ w\ \times\ 3 \qquad [\text{because } \sigma_{p_0}\ v = \sigma_{p_0}\ w] \\
&= f_1\ w \\
&= \sigma_{p_1}\ (f_1\ w)
\end{aligned}
$$

and the case of V_2 is as easy. But, even though the division is congruent it would cause problems for most partial evaluators. Congruence only examines f_1 in the restricted context in which it will actually be called, and not over the whole domain of values. This means that divisions may take into account implications from surrounding conditionals and still be congruent. Thus f_1 is allowed to "know" that its parameter y will have value 3. If a division takes advantage of this then so must the specialisation algorithm—it must perform either driving or generalised partial computation [FN88]. What is more, *all* the information implied by the conditional must be extracted and used in case the division has taken advantage of it. In general this is uncomputable. If, on the other hand, the specialisation is performed by an ordinary partial evaluator then the division will act as if it were not congruent.

In practice problems do not occur as a far stronger version of congruence, namely *intensional congruence*, is normally used. However, this is defined syntactically rather than semantically which makes it heavily language dependent.

It is possible to revise the definition of congruence so that it loses this value dependence but otherwise remains the same. In the definition of control structures the functions $\{f_i\}$ were only defined on the particular V_i, and so it only made sense to draw the values v and w from V_i. This led to value dependence. There is actually no reason why the functions $\{f_i\}$ should not be defined over the whole of the value domain V. After all, that is the range of their definition in the program. The original $\{f_i\}$ are just restricted versions of these. Let us now use $\{f_i\}$ to denote the unrestricted versions, so that $f_i : V \to V$ for each i. Now we can define a value independent, or uniform, variant of congruence which we shall call *uniform congruence*.

Definition
A division (σ, δ, π) is *uniformly congruent* at a program point p with respect to a control structure $\{(V_i,\ f_i : V \to V)\}$ if for each i,

$$\forall v, w \in V \ . \ \sigma_p\ v = \sigma_p\ w \ \Rightarrow \ \sigma_{p_i}\ (f_i\ v) = \sigma_{p_i}\ (f_i\ w)$$

Note that, unlike the definition of congruence, the values v and w are free to range over the whole of V. As this is a stronger condition than congruence, uniformly congruent divisions are also congruent, but a congruent division is only uniformly congruent if *any* two values with equal static parts are given equal static parts by f_i.

3.5   Safety ⇔ Uniform Congruence

In order to compare uniform congruence and safety we have to make a small extension to the revised program model. The definition of nx assumes that it will always be possible to determine which program point is the destination. This is not unreasonable in an iterative language where the value v is computed using built in operators only. In a recursive language, the computation of v may be given by user defined functions and so may not terminate. Then $nx\ (p, v)$ will be undefined. This must be reflected in the control structure. We add a new program point $p_\perp$ and define $nx\ (p_\perp, v) = (p_\perp, v)$ for all values $v \in V$. Adding an ordering where $p_\perp \sqsubseteq p$ for all $p \in P$ makes P into a (flat) domain. V likewise becomes a domain and the $\{V_i\}$ disjoint open sets in V. The rest of V (that is, $V \setminus \bigcup \{V_i\}$) is a closed set which we will call $V_\perp$. Finally we define the transfer function $f_\perp : V \to V$ by $f_\perp\ v = \perp$. So, if $v \in V_i$ for some $i(\neq \perp)$, then $nx\ (p, v) = (p_i, f_i\ v)$ as before, but if $v \in V_\perp$ then $nx\ (p, v) = (p_\perp, \perp)$ and the value of the program is $\perp$. Notice that $V_\perp$ may be empty at some program points.

At every program point $f_\perp\ v = \perp$, so a division which is congruent with respect to some control structure will still be congruent if we extend the control structure with $V_\perp$. This means that we can be a little sloppy with our notation. We will typically include $V_\perp$ in the $\{V_i\}$.

Definition
A division (σ, δ, π) is *safe* at a program point p with respect to a control structure $\{(V_i,\ f_i : V \to V)\}$ if for each i, $\sigma_{p_i} \circ f_i = \sigma_{p_i} \circ f_i \circ \sigma_p$

The extension to the program model is required because it is possible for a projection σ to map a value from a set V_i into $V_\perp$. Having defined safety we can now prove that it is equivalent to uniform congruence.

Theorem 3.1
Let $\Delta\ (= (\sigma, \delta, \pi))$ be a division. Δ is safe if, and only if, it is uniformly congruent.

Proof
Assume Δ is safe. Let p be a program point and let $\{(V_i,\ f_i : V \to V)\}$ be the control structure at p. As Δ is safe we know that $\sigma_{p_i} \circ f_i = \sigma_{p_i} \circ f_i \circ \sigma_p$ for each i. We want to prove that if $\sigma_p\ v = \sigma_p\ w$ then $\sigma_{p_i}\ (f_i\ v) = \sigma_{p_i}\ (f_i\ w)$ for all i and $v, w \in V$. So, assume that $\sigma_p\ v = \sigma_p\ w$ for some arbitrary i and $v, w \in V$. Then,

$$
\begin{aligned}
\sigma_{p_i}\ (f_i\ v) &= (\sigma_{p_i} \circ f_i)\ v \\
&= (\sigma_{p_i} \circ f_i \circ \sigma_p)\ v && \text{[safety]} \\
&= (\sigma_{p_i} \circ f_i)\ (\sigma_p\ v) \\
&= (\sigma_{p_i} \circ f_i)\ (\sigma_p\ w) && \text{[by assumption]} \\
&= (\sigma_{p_i} \circ f_i \circ \sigma_p)\ w \\
&= (\sigma_{p_i} \circ f_i)\ w && \text{[safety]} \\
&= \sigma_{p_i}\ (f_i\ w)
\end{aligned}
$$

and so Δ is uniformly congruent a p.

Conversely, assume Δ is uniformly congruent. Let p be a program point and let $\{(V_i,\ f_i : V \to V)\}$ be the control structure at p. The projection σ_p is idempotent so $\sigma_p\ v = \sigma_p\ (\sigma_p\ v)$ for any value $v \in V$. As the division is uniformly congruent we may conclude that $\sigma_{p_i}\ (f_i\ v) = \sigma_{p_i}\ (f_i\ (\sigma_p\ v))$ for any value $v \in V$. In other words, $\sigma_{p_i} \circ f_i = \sigma_{p_i} \circ f_i \circ \sigma_p$ as required. $\square$

We have seen, at least in principle, that projections may be used to provide descriptions of program values, pinpointing which parts are static. Furthermore, the safety condition used in strictness analysis is precisely the condition needed to ensure uniform congruence. What we must do now is to provide both concrete and abstract semantics for some particular language to verify that the principle of using projections is realisable in practice. This is done in the next chapter.

Chapter 4

Binding-Time Analysis

In this chapter we explore some of the practicalities of using projections in binding-time analysis of typed lazy functional languages. We have chosen typed languages because we use type information to control the structure of the projections. For concreteness we define a simplified language and with its aid present the binding-time analysis equations. We demonstrate their safety, and show that an approximation to the analysis may be performed in a finite time.

4.1 PEL Abstract Syntax

The language PEL (Partial Evaluation Language) is intended as a toy language only but is very much in the style of other lazy functional languages. Unlike "realistic" languages it has no predefined types like *integer* or *character* and without the addition of certain standard features it would be impractical to use regularly. However the programmer is able to define arbitrary algebraic data types so it is possible to write fairly complex programs.

The advantage in restricting ourselves to a simple language is that we should be able to avoid being swamped by unnecessary detail. What we learn from discussing it can be applied to larger languages.

A variety of syntactic classes appear in the grammar that follows. Single (subscripted/decorated) letters represent variables in the various classes.

e	∈	*Expr*	[Expressions]
x	∈	*Var*	[Variables]
f	∈	*Fun*	[Functions]
c	∈	*Con*	[Constructors]
d	∈	*Fndefn*	[Function Definitions]
p	∈	*Prog*	[Programs]
T	∈	*Type*	[Types]
A	∈	*Alg*	[Algebraic Types]
D	∈	*Tdefn*	[Type Definitions]
C	∈	*Tdecl*	[Function Type Declarations]

So, for example, program variables will be called x, x_i etc. Rather than continually distinguish between individual variables and vectors of variables we will assume that, typically, x represents a vector of variables. When we do need to describe the ith variable from a vector x we will use the notation $x(i)$.

A program consists of a series of type definitions followed by some function definitions, each of which is immediately preceded by a declaration of its type. The program concludes with an expression and its associated type. The expression represents the meaning of the program in the context of the preceding declarations. We use {*pattern*} to signify zero or more repetitions.

```
p  →  {D} {C d} e::T
d  →  f x = e;
e  →  x
   |  (e₁,...,eₙ)
   |  c e
   |  f e
   |  case e in c₁ x₁ -> e₁ || ... || cₙ xₙ -> eₙ end
D  →  A = c T {+ c T};
C  →  f :: T -> T;
T  →  A
   |  (T₁,...,Tₙ)
```

An example program will make the grammar easier to follow. To make programs easier to read, some constructors (e.g. `False`) are not given an argument. When the argument to a constructor is omitted it is assumed to be the empty tuple () which represents the element of the void (or unit) type. We will write either () or **1** to denote this type.

```
Bool ::= False + True;

and :: (Bool,Bool) -> Bool;
and (x,y) = case x in
                  False -> False
            || True  -> y
            end;

and (and (True,False), True) :: Bool
```

4.2   Type Rules

We will assume the program satisfies various well-formedness criteria in addition to syntactic correctness. For example, no function should be defined twice, the constructors in a **case** expression should all be from the same type, and so on. In addition a program must be well-typed. PEL is first-order and, at this juncture, monomorphic, but by using the algebraic type definitions PEL allows for the definition of new types using (separated) sum, (standard) product and recursion. Explicit type declarations are provided for the functions, so the type of any expression may be easily inferred.

We use the variables R, S and T to represent types and write assumptions of the form $x::T$ to mean $x(1)::T(1),\ldots,x(n)::T(n)$. The assumption lists only contain details about the local variables within a function body. A typing judgement concerning a function is true exactly when it accords with the type declaration given in the program. The same is true of constructors. If a constructor c_i appears in the definition of a type S then S is of the form $S = c_1\ S_1 + \cdots + c_n\ S_n$ for some types $\{S_i\}_{i=1}^{n}$ and $c_i::S_i\text{->}S$ as usual. The typing rules for expressions are as follows.

$$x::T \ \vdash \ x(i)::T(i)$$

$$\frac{x::T \vdash e_1::R_1 \quad \cdots \quad x::T \vdash e_n::R_n}{x::T \ \vdash \ (e_1,\ldots,e_n)::(R_1,\ldots,R_n)}$$

$$\frac{\text{f::R->S} \qquad \text{x::T} \vdash \text{e::R}}{\text{x::T} \vdash \text{f e::S}}$$

$$\frac{\text{c}_i\text{::S}_i\text{->S} \qquad \text{x::T} \vdash \text{e::S}_i}{\text{x::T} \vdash \text{c}_i \text{ e::S}}$$

$$\frac{\text{x::T} \vdash \text{e::S} \qquad \forall i . (\text{x::T}, \text{y}_i\text{::S}_i \vdash \text{e}_i\text{::R})}{\text{x::T} \vdash \text{case e in c}_1 \text{ y}_1 \text{ -> e}_1 \mid\mid \dots \mid\mid \text{c}_n \text{ y}_n \text{ -> e}_n \text{ end::R}}$$

Only well-formed and well-typed programs are assigned a meaning. This meaning is defined by the denotational semantics.

4.3 Denotational Semantics

The denotational semantics is fairly standard. There are three semantic domains—one to model values and the other two to model value and function environments respectively. The function environment is kept separate because functions are not values—all functions are first-order.

$$
\begin{aligned}
v &\in Value &=& (Con \times Value) + (Value \times Value) \\
\rho &\in Venv &=& Var \rightarrow Value \\
\phi &\in Fenv &=& Fun \rightarrow (Value \rightarrow Value)
\end{aligned}
$$

While we use a universal value domain it is often useful to imagine otherwise. For example, if we have a program function f with type $X\text{->}Y$ it is convenient to think of its meaning f as being a function $f : X \rightarrow Y$ where the domain X corresponds to the type X and likewise with Y. We can make this more precise. Using domain sum, product and limit we can construct domains to correspond with the type definitions and can construct the obvious projection pairs between these domains and the universal value domain. Thus if X is a type with corresponding domain X, there exist maps $\phi_X : X \rightarrow Value$ and $\psi_X : Value \rightarrow X$ such that $\psi_X \circ \phi_X = ID_X$ and $\phi_X \circ \psi_X \sqsubseteq ID_{Value}$. Then any value $x \in X$ may be identified with a unique $v \in Value$ given by $v = \phi_X(x)$. This means that we can ignore the distinction between elements in X and elements in $Value$ lying in the range of ϕ_X. We do not prove that our *typed programs cannot go wrong* [Mil78] but the proof would be similar to Milner's.

There are two semantic functions. The first constructs a function environment from the function definitions. The second assigns meanings to expressions in a context supplied by the function and value environments. There are no predefined functions so the function environment is constructed from the program's function definitions only.

$$\mathcal{D} \; : \; \textit{Fndefn}^* \; \rightarrow \; \textit{Fenv}$$

$$\mathcal{D}[\![\, \mathbf{f}_1 \; \mathbf{x}_1 \; = \; \mathbf{e}_1 \, , \ldots, \; \mathbf{f}_n \; \mathbf{x}_n \; = \; \mathbf{e}_n \,]\!]$$
$$= \; \textit{fix} \; (\lambda \phi \, . \, \{ \mathbf{f}_1 \mapsto \lambda v . \mathcal{E}_\phi[\![\, \mathbf{e}_1 \,]\!]_{\{x_1 \mapsto v\}} \, , \ldots, \; \mathbf{f}_n \mapsto \lambda v . \mathcal{E}_\phi[\![\, \mathbf{e}_n \,]\!]_{\{x_n \mapsto v\}} \})$$

$$\mathcal{E} \; : \; \textit{Fenv} \; \rightarrow \; \textit{Expr} \; \rightarrow \; \textit{Venv} \; \rightarrow \; \textit{Value}$$

$$\mathcal{E}_\phi[\![\, \mathbf{x} \,]\!]_\rho \qquad = \quad \rho[\![\, \mathbf{x} \,]\!]$$

$$\mathcal{E}_\phi[\![\, (\mathbf{e}_1, \ldots, \mathbf{e}_n) \,]\!]_\rho \quad = \quad (\mathcal{E}_\phi[\![\, \mathbf{e}_1 \,]\!]_\rho, \ldots, \mathcal{E}_\phi[\![\, \mathbf{e}_n \,]\!]_\rho)$$

$$\mathcal{E}_\phi[\![\, \mathbf{c} \; \mathbf{e} \,]\!]_\rho \qquad = \quad c \; (\mathcal{E}_\phi[\![\, \mathbf{e} \,]\!]_\rho)$$

$$\mathcal{E}_\phi[\![\, \mathbf{f} \; \mathbf{e} \,]\!]_\rho \qquad = \quad \phi[\![\, \mathbf{f} \,]\!] \; (\mathcal{E}_\phi[\![\, \mathbf{e} \,]\!]_\rho)$$

$$\mathcal{E}_\phi[\![\, \mathtt{case} \; \mathbf{e} \; \mathtt{in} \; \mathbf{c}_1 \; \mathbf{x}_1 \; \mathtt{\text{-}>} \; \mathbf{e}_1 \; \mathtt{||} \; \ldots \; \mathtt{||} \; \mathbf{c}_n \; \mathbf{x}_n \; \mathtt{\text{-}>} \; \mathbf{e}_n \; \mathtt{end} \,]\!]_\rho$$
$$= \quad \textit{case} \; \mathcal{E}_\phi[\![\, \mathbf{e} \,]\!]_\rho \; \textit{in}$$
$$c_1 \; v_1 \quad \Rightarrow \quad \mathcal{E}_\phi[\![\, \mathbf{e}_1 \,]\!]_{\rho \oplus \{x_1 \mapsto v_1\}}$$
$$\vdots$$
$$c_n \; v_n \quad \Rightarrow \quad \mathcal{E}_\phi[\![\, \mathbf{e}_n \,]\!]_{\rho \oplus \{x_n \mapsto v_n\}}$$

The operator $\oplus$ combines environments. It is defined by,

$$(\rho \oplus \rho') \; x \; = \; \begin{cases} \rho' \, x & \text{if defined} \\ \rho \, x & \text{otherwise} \end{cases}$$

So $\rho \oplus \rho'$ is ρ overridden by ρ'. The form $\{x \mapsto v\}$ represents a function element in the usual way, but as x is in general a vector of variables, this means $\{x(1) \mapsto \textit{fst} \; v, \; x(2) \mapsto \textit{snd} \; v, \ldots \}$. We will use this notation freely on environments of any type.

The functions in the program can be mutually recursive. This is captured in $\mathcal{D}$ through the use of *fix*. The fixed point is taken across all the function definitions simultaneously. In $\mathcal{E}$, certain values need to be appropriately injected into *Value* using the device discussed earlier. For example, the meaning of the constructed term $c \; (\mathcal{E}_\phi[\![\, \mathbf{e} \,]\!]_\rho)$ is really given by the value $\textit{inl} \; (c, \mathcal{E}_\phi[\![\, \mathbf{e} \,]\!]_\rho)$ in *Value*. Finally we notice the distinction between the syntactic "case" and the semantic "*case*" in the definition of

$\mathcal{E}$. We assume the latter to be the standard mathematical function but are providing a definition for the former.

Explicitly writing $\mathcal{E}_\phi[\![\,\mathbf{e}\,]\!]_\rho$ for the meaning of an expression $\mathbf{e}$, and $\phi[\![\,\mathbf{f}\,]\!]$ for the meaning of a function $\mathbf{f}$ is cumbersome. There are times when we will need to be precise in this way. Otherwise, when ϕ is the full function environment defined by $\mathcal{D}$, we will just write f for $\phi[\![\,\mathbf{f}\,]\!]$ and $e_{[v/x]}$ for $\mathcal{E}_\phi[\![\,\mathbf{e}\,]\!]_{\{x\mapsto v\}}$.

4.4 Abstract Semantics

We define an abstract semantics for PEL. The abstract values are projections over the universal value domain. As before there are two environments, one for abstract values and the other for abstract functions. We will follow Mycroft's notation [Myc81] and use a $\#$ superscript to indicate the abstract interpretation.

$$
\begin{array}{rcll}
\gamma & \in & Proj & = & Value \overset{proj}{\to} Value & \text{[domain of finitary projections]} \\
\rho^\# & \in & AbsVenv & = & Var \to Proj \\
\phi^\# & \in & AbsFenv & = & Fun \to (Proj \to Proj)
\end{array}
$$

The greatest lower bound of two projections within the domain of functions (as given by $\gamma \sqcap \delta = \lambda x.\gamma\; x \sqcap \delta\; x$) is not, in general, a projection. However, greatest lower bounds do exist in $Value \overset{proj}{\to} Value$ for the following reason. Projections are bounded by ID, so the set of projections $\{\beta \mid \beta \sqsubseteq \gamma \wedge \beta \sqsubseteq \delta\}$ is consistent and, hence, its least upper bound exists. This least upper bound is a finitary projection and is greater than all other lower bounds for γ and δ and so it is the greatest lower bound.

The difference between these different greatest lower bounds becomes irrelevant when we introduce particular finite domains of projections, as in these domains, the usual greatest lower bound of any set of projections from these domains is itself a projection and, moreover, also a member of the same finite domain.

Using the same trick as before we can identify projections over a domain X with projections in $Proj$. Write $Proj_X$ for the projections on X. Then there exist functions $\Phi_X : Proj_X \to Proj$ and $\Psi_X : Proj \to Proj_X$ such that $\Psi_X \circ \Phi_X = ID_{Proj_X}$ and

$\Phi_X \circ \Psi_X \sqsubseteq ID_{Proj}$. Φ_X and Ψ_X can be defined using the projection pair ϕ_X, ψ_X of the previous section.

$$\Phi_X = \lambda\gamma . \phi_X \circ \gamma \circ \psi_X$$
$$\Psi_X = \lambda\beta . \psi_X \circ \beta \circ \phi_X$$

Therefore, as with values, we need not distinguish notationally between a projection in $Proj_X$ and the corresponding projection in $Proj$.

We need to define product and sum operations on projections.

Definition

If $\{\gamma_i : X_i \to X_i\}_{\{1 \le i \le n\}}$ is a family of projections, then we define the projection $(\gamma_1 \times \cdots \times \gamma_n) : (X_1, \ldots, X_n) \to (X_1, \ldots, X_n)$ by

$$(\gamma_1 \times \cdots \times \gamma_n)(x_1, \ldots, x_n) = (\gamma_1\, x_1, \ldots, \gamma_n\, x_n)$$

Definition

If $\{\gamma_i : X_i \to X_i\}_{\{1 \le i \le n\}}$ is a family of projections, then we define the projection $(c_1\, \gamma_1 + \cdots + c_n\, \gamma_n) : (c_1\, X_1 + \cdots + c_n\, X_n) \to (c_1\, X_1 + \cdots + c_n\, X_n)$ by

$$(c_1\, \gamma_1 + \cdots + c_n\, \gamma_n)\ \bot\ =\ \bot$$
$$(c_1\, \gamma_1 + \cdots + c_n\, \gamma_n)\ (c_1\, x_1)\ =\ c_1\,(\gamma_1\, x_1)$$
$$\vdots$$
$$(c_1\, \gamma_1 + \cdots + c_n\, \gamma_n)\ (c_n\, x_n)\ =\ c_n\,(\gamma_n\, x_n)$$

We will sometimes use the more convenient notation $\sum_i (c_i\, \gamma_i)$ as a short form for $(c_1\, \gamma_1 + \cdots + c_n\, \gamma_n)$.

There are two abstract semantic functions. These evaluate functions and expressions in the abstract domains and correspond directly with the concrete semantic functions.

$$\mathcal{D}^\# : \mathit{Fndefn}^* \to \mathit{AbsFenv}$$
$$\mathcal{D}^\#[\![\mathbf{f}_1\ \mathbf{x}_1 = \mathbf{e}_1 , \ldots, \mathbf{f}_n\ \mathbf{x}_n = \mathbf{e}_n]\!]$$
$$=\ \mathit{gfp}\,(\lambda\phi^\# . \{\mathbf{f}_1 \mapsto \lambda v.\mathcal{E}^\#_{\phi^\#}[\![\mathbf{e}_1]\!]_{\{x_1 \mapsto v\}}, \ldots, \mathbf{f}_n \mapsto \lambda v.\mathcal{E}^\#_{\phi^\#}[\![\mathbf{e}_n]\!]_{\{x_n \mapsto v\}} \})$$

$$\mathcal{E}^{\#} \; : \; AbsFenv \; \rightarrow \; Expr \; \rightarrow \; AbsVenv \; \rightarrow \; Proj$$

$$\mathcal{E}^{\#}_{\phi^{\#}}[\![\, x \,]\!]_{\rho^{\#}} \quad = \quad \rho^{\#}\,[\![\, x \,]\!]$$

$$\mathcal{E}^{\#}_{\phi^{\#}}[\![\, (e_1,\dots,e_n) \,]\!]_{\rho^{\#}} \quad = \quad \mathcal{E}^{\#}_{\phi^{\#}}[\![\, e_1 \,]\!]_{\rho^{\#}} \times \cdots \times \mathcal{E}^{\#}_{\phi^{\#}}[\![\, e_n \,]\!]_{\rho^{\#}}$$

$$\mathcal{E}^{\#}_{\phi^{\#}}[\![\, c_k \; e \,]\!]_{\rho^{\#}} \quad = \quad c_1 \; ID + \cdots + c_k \; (\mathcal{E}^{\#}_{\phi^{\#}}[\![\, e \,]\!]_{\rho^{\#}}) + \cdots + c_n \; ID$$

$$\mathcal{E}^{\#}_{\phi^{\#}}[\![\, f \; e \,]\!]_{\rho^{\#}} \quad = \quad \phi^{\#}\,[\![\, f \,]\!]\,(\mathcal{E}^{\#}_{\phi^{\#}}[\![\, e \,]\!]_{\rho^{\#}})$$

$$\mathcal{E}^{\#}_{\phi^{\#}}[\![\, \text{case } e \text{ in } c_1 \; x_1 \; \text{->} \; e_1 \; |\!| \; \dots \; |\!| \; c_n \; x_n \; \text{->} \; e_n \text{ end} \,]\!]_{\rho^{\#}}$$

$$= \quad case \; \mathcal{E}^{\#}_{\phi^{\#}}[\![\, e \,]\!]_{\rho^{\#}} \; in$$

$$\textstyle\sum_i (c_i \; \gamma_i) \;\Rightarrow\; \bigsqcap_i (\mathcal{E}^{\#}_{\phi^{\#}}[\![\, e_i \,]\!]_{\rho^{\#} \oplus \{x_i \mapsto \gamma_i\}})$$

$$else \quad\Rightarrow\quad ABS$$

The only projections which preserve all the tags of their arguments are of the form $\sum_i (c_i \; \gamma_i)$, so it is only in this case that we can be sure of being able to select which branch the case will take. Any other projection (which must map at least one tag to $\perp$) will be treated as if it were ABS (which maps all tags to $\perp$).[1]

Initially surprising, in the definition of $\mathcal{D}^{\#}$, is the use of greatest fixed point (gfp). Actually any fixed point is safe but, as we noted in Chapter 3 (Section 2.1), in contrast with backwards analysis, larger projections give more accurate information. As with the concrete semantics we will sometimes use an abbreviated notation. When $\phi^{\#}$ is the result of $\mathcal{D}^{\#}$ applied to the whole program, we will write $f^{\#}$ for $\phi^{\#}[\![\, f \,]\!]$, and $e^{\#}_{[\gamma/x]}$ for $\mathcal{E}^{\#}_{\phi^{\#}}[\![\, e \,]\!]_{\{x \mapsto \gamma\}}$.

Before we give the binding-time equations and prove them correct we will demonstrate that the abstract semantics are indeed a safe abstraction of the concrete semantics.

Lemma 4.1
If ϕ and $\phi^{\#}$ are function environments for which $\phi^{\#}[\![\, f \,]\!] \; \gamma \circ \phi[\![\, f \,]\!] \sqsubseteq \phi[\![\, f \,]\!] \circ \gamma$ for all function names f and all projections γ (of the appropriate type) then

$$\mathcal{E}^{\#}_{\phi^{\#}}[\![\, e \,]\!]_{\{x \mapsto \gamma\}} \circ \lambda v.\mathcal{E}_{\phi}[\![\, e \,]\!]_{\{x \mapsto v\}} \sqsubseteq \lambda v.\mathcal{E}_{\phi}[\![\, e \,]\!]_{\{x \mapsto v\}} \circ \gamma$$

Proof
The proof is by induction over the structure of e. We will prove the equivalent

---

[1] When we introduce finite domains of projections in Section 4.7, the only projections over sum domains that we consider are either ABS or are of the form $\sum_i (c_i \; \gamma_i)$.

result, that $(\mathcal{E}^{\#}_{\phi\#}[\![\,e\,]\!]_{\{x\mapsto\gamma\}})\,(\mathcal{E}_{\phi}[\![\,e\,]\!]_{\{x\mapsto v\}})\sqsubseteq\mathcal{E}_{\phi}[\![\,e\,]\!]_{\{x\mapsto\gamma v\}}$ for all values v (obtained by applying both sides to v).

Case: $(\mathtt{x(i)})$

$$
\begin{aligned}
&(\mathcal{E}^{\#}_{\phi\#}[\![\,\mathtt{x(i)}\,]\!]_{\{x\mapsto\gamma\}})\,(\mathcal{E}_{\phi}[\![\,\mathtt{x(i)}\,]\!]_{\{x\mapsto v\}})\\
&=\quad \gamma(i)\ v(i)\\
&=\quad \mathcal{E}_{\phi}[\![\,\mathtt{x(i)}\,]\!]_{\{x\mapsto\gamma v\}}
\end{aligned}
$$

Case: $(\mathtt{e}_1,\ldots,\mathtt{e}_n)$

$$
\begin{aligned}
&(\mathcal{E}^{\#}_{\phi\#}[\![\,(\mathtt{e}_1,\ldots,\mathtt{e}_n)\,]\!]_{\{x\mapsto\gamma\}})\,(\mathcal{E}_{\phi}[\![\,(\mathtt{e}_1,\ldots,\mathtt{e}_n)\,]\!]_{\{x\mapsto v\}})\\
&=\quad (\mathcal{E}^{\#}_{\phi\#}[\![\,\mathtt{e}_1\,]\!]_{\{x\mapsto\gamma\}}\times\cdots\times\mathcal{E}^{\#}_{\phi\#}[\![\,\mathtt{e}_n\,]\!]_{\{x\mapsto\gamma\}})\,(\mathcal{E}_{\phi}[\![\,\mathtt{e}_1\,]\!]_{\{x\mapsto v\}},\ldots,\mathcal{E}_{\phi}[\![\,\mathtt{e}_1\,]\!]_{\{x\mapsto v\}})\\
&=\quad ((\mathcal{E}^{\#}_{\phi\#}[\![\,\mathtt{e}_1\,]\!]_{\{x\mapsto\gamma\}})\,(\mathcal{E}_{\phi}[\![\,\mathtt{e}_1\,]\!]_{\{x\mapsto v\}}),\ldots,(\mathcal{E}^{\#}_{\phi\#}[\![\,\mathtt{e}_n\,]\!]_{\{x\mapsto\gamma\}})\,(\mathcal{E}_{\phi}[\![\,\mathtt{e}_n\,]\!]_{\{x\mapsto v\}}))\\
&\sqsubseteq\quad (\mathcal{E}_{\phi}[\![\,\mathtt{e}_1\,]\!]_{\{x\mapsto\gamma v\}},\ldots,\mathcal{E}_{\phi}[\![\,\mathtt{e}_n\,]\!]_{\{x\mapsto\gamma v\}})\qquad\text{[induction]}\\
&=\quad \mathcal{E}_{\phi}[\![\,(\mathtt{e}_1,\ldots,\mathtt{e}_n)\,]\!]_{\{x\mapsto\gamma v\}}
\end{aligned}
$$

Case: $(\mathtt{c}_k\ \mathtt{e})$

$$
\begin{aligned}
&(\mathcal{E}^{\#}_{\phi\#}[\![\,\mathtt{c}_k\ \mathtt{e}\,]\!]_{\{x\mapsto\gamma\}})\,(\mathcal{E}_{\phi}[\![\,\mathtt{c}_k\ \mathtt{e}\,]\!]_{\{x\mapsto v\}})\\
&=\quad (c_1\ ID+\cdots+c_k\ (\mathcal{E}^{\#}_{\phi\#}[\![\,\mathtt{e}\,]\!]_{\{x\mapsto\gamma\}})+\cdots+c_n\ ID)\,(c_k\ \mathcal{E}_{\phi}[\![\,\mathtt{e}\,]\!]_{\{x\mapsto v\}})\\
&=\quad c_k\ ((\mathcal{E}^{\#}_{\phi\#}[\![\,\mathtt{e}\,]\!]_{\{x\mapsto\gamma\}})\,(\mathcal{E}_{\phi}[\![\,\mathtt{e}\,]\!]_{\{x\mapsto v\}}))\\
&\sqsubseteq\quad c_k\ (\mathcal{E}_{\phi}[\![\,\mathtt{e}\,]\!]_{\{x\mapsto\gamma v\}})\qquad\text{[induction]}\\
&=\quad \mathcal{E}_{\phi}[\![\,\mathtt{c}_k\ \mathtt{e}\,]\!]_{\{x\mapsto\gamma v\}}
\end{aligned}
$$

Case: $(\mathtt{f}\ \mathtt{e})$

$$
\begin{aligned}
&(\mathcal{E}^{\#}_{\phi\#}[\![\,\mathtt{f}\ \mathtt{e}\,]\!]_{\{x\mapsto\gamma\}})\,(\mathcal{E}_{\phi}[\![\,\mathtt{f}\ \mathtt{e}\,]\!]_{\{x\mapsto v\}})\\
&=\quad (\phi^{\#}[\![\,\mathtt{f}\,]\!]\,(\mathcal{E}^{\#}_{\phi\#}[\![\,\mathtt{e}\,]\!]_{\{x\mapsto\gamma\}}))\,(\phi[\![\,\mathtt{f}\,]\!]\,(\mathcal{E}_{\phi}[\![\,\mathtt{e}\,]\!]_{\{x\mapsto v\}}))\\
&\sqsubseteq\quad \phi[\![\,\mathtt{f}\,]\!]\,((\mathcal{E}^{\#}_{\phi\#}[\![\,\mathtt{e}\,]\!]_{\{x\mapsto\gamma\}})\,(\mathcal{E}_{\phi}[\![\,\mathtt{e}\,]\!]_{\{x\mapsto v\}}))\qquad\text{[assumption]}\\
&\sqsubseteq\quad \phi[\![\,\mathtt{f}\,]\!]\,(\mathcal{E}_{\phi}[\![\,\mathtt{e}\,]\!]_{\{x\mapsto\gamma v\}})\qquad\text{[induction]}\\
&=\quad \mathcal{E}_{\phi}[\![\,\mathtt{f}\ \mathtt{e}\,]\!]_{\{x\mapsto\gamma v\}})
\end{aligned}
$$

Case: $(\mathtt{case}\ \mathtt{e}\ \mathtt{in}\ \ldots\ \mathtt{c}_k\ \mathtt{x}_k\ \mathtt{\text{->}}\ \mathtt{e}_k\ \ldots\ \mathtt{end})$
The (projection valued) result of $\mathcal{E}^{\#}_{\phi\#}[\![\,\mathtt{case}\ \mathtt{e}\ \mathtt{in}\ \ldots\ \mathtt{c}_k\ \mathtt{x}_k\ \mathtt{\text{->}}\ \mathtt{e}_k\ \ldots\ \mathtt{end}\,]\!]_{\{x\mapsto\gamma\}}$ is

expressed as a case statement with two possibilities. We will consider these two possibilities in reverse order. So, the first possibility is that $\mathcal{E}^{\#}_{\phi\#}[\![\,e\,]\!]_{\{x\mapsto\gamma\}}$ is not of the form $\sum_i (c_i\ \gamma_i)$, in which case $\mathcal{E}^{\#}_{\phi\#}[\![\,\texttt{case e in} \ldots \texttt{c}_k\ \texttt{x}_k \ \texttt{->}\ \texttt{e}_k \ldots \texttt{end}\,]\!]_{\{x\mapsto\gamma\}} = ABS$ and,

$$
\begin{aligned}
&ABS\ (\mathcal{E}_{\phi}[\![\,\texttt{case e in} \ldots \texttt{c}_k\ \texttt{x}_k \ \texttt{->}\ \texttt{e}_k \ldots \texttt{end}\,]\!]_{\{x\mapsto v\}}) \\
&= \bot \\
&\sqsubseteq\ \mathcal{E}_{\phi}[\![\,\texttt{case e in} \ldots \texttt{c}_k\ \texttt{x}_k \ \texttt{->}\ \texttt{e}_k \ldots \texttt{end}\,]\!]_{\{x\mapsto\gamma v\}}
\end{aligned}
$$

The other possibility to consider is that $\mathcal{E}^{\#}_{\phi\#}[\![\,e\,]\!]_{\{x\mapsto\gamma\}} = \sum_i c_i\ \gamma_i$. If this is the case then $\mathcal{E}^{\#}_{\phi\#}[\![\,\texttt{case e in} \ldots \texttt{c}_k\ \texttt{x}_k \ \texttt{->e}_k \ldots \texttt{end}\,]\!]_{\{x\mapsto\gamma\}} = \bigsqcap_i (\mathcal{E}^{\#}_{\phi\#}[\![\,e_i\,]\!]_{\{x\mapsto\gamma,x_i\mapsto\gamma_i\}})$ and the calculation proceeds as follows.

$$
(\bigsqcap_i \mathcal{E}^{\#}_{\phi\#}[\![\,e_i\,]\!]_{\{x\mapsto\gamma,x_i\mapsto\gamma_i\}})\ (\mathcal{E}_{\phi}[\![\,\texttt{case e in} \ldots \texttt{c}_k\ \texttt{x}_k \ \texttt{->}\ \texttt{e}_k \ldots \texttt{end}\,]\!]_{\{x\mapsto v\}})
$$

$$
= (\bigsqcap_i \mathcal{E}^{\#}_{\phi\#}[\![\,e_i\,]\!]_{\{x\mapsto\gamma,x_i\mapsto\gamma_i\}}) \left(
\begin{array}{l}
case\ \mathcal{E}_{\phi}[\![\,e\,]\!]_{\{x\mapsto v\}}\ in \\
\qquad\vdots \\
c_k\ y_k\ \Rightarrow\ \mathcal{E}_{\phi}[\![\,e_k\,]\!]_{\{x\mapsto v, x_k\mapsto y_k\}} \\
\qquad\vdots
\end{array}
\right)
$$

$$
\begin{aligned}
\sqsubseteq\quad & case\ \mathcal{E}_{\phi}[\![\,e\,]\!]_{\{x\mapsto v\}}\ in \\
& \qquad\vdots \\
& c_k\ y_k\ \Rightarrow\ (\mathcal{E}^{\#}_{\phi\#}[\![\,e_k\,]\!]_{\{x\mapsto\gamma,x_k\mapsto\gamma_k\}})\ (\mathcal{E}_{\phi}[\![\,e_k\,]\!]_{\{x\mapsto v,x_k\mapsto y_k\}}) \\
& \qquad\vdots
\end{aligned}
$$

$$
\begin{aligned}
\sqsubseteq\quad & case\ \mathcal{E}_{\phi}[\![\,e\,]\!]_{\{x\mapsto v\}}\ in \qquad\qquad \text{[induction]} \\
& \qquad\vdots \\
& c_k\ y_k\ \Rightarrow\ \mathcal{E}_{\phi}[\![\,e_k\,]\!]_{\{x\mapsto\gamma v, x_k\mapsto\gamma_k y_k\}} \\
& \qquad\vdots
\end{aligned}
$$

$$
\begin{aligned}
=\quad & case\ (\sum_i c_i\ \gamma_i)\ (\mathcal{E}_{\phi}[\![\,e\,]\!]_{\{x\mapsto v\}})\ in \qquad \text{[meaning of } case\text{]} \\
& \qquad\vdots \\
& c_k\ y_k\ \Rightarrow\ \mathcal{E}_{\phi}[\![\,e_k\,]\!]_{\{x\mapsto\gamma v, x_k\mapsto y_k\}} \\
& \qquad\vdots
\end{aligned}
$$

$$= \quad case \; (\mathcal{E}^{\#}_{\phi^{\#}}[\![\, e \,]\!]_{\{x \mapsto \gamma\}}) \; (\mathcal{E}_{\phi}[\![\, e \,]\!]_{\{x \mapsto v\}}) \; in$$

$$\vdots$$

$$c_k \; y_k \quad \Rightarrow \quad \mathcal{E}_{\phi}[\![\, e_k \,]\!]_{\{x \mapsto \gamma v, x_k \mapsto y_k\}}$$

$$\vdots$$

$$\sqsubseteq \quad case \; \mathcal{E}_{\phi}[\![\, e \,]\!]_{\{x \mapsto \gamma v\}} \; in \qquad\qquad\qquad\qquad\qquad \text{[induction]}$$

$$\vdots$$

$$c_k \; y_k \quad \Rightarrow \quad \mathcal{E}_{\phi}[\![\, e_k \,]\!]_{\{x \mapsto \gamma v, x_k \mapsto y_k\}}$$

$$\vdots$$

$$= \quad \mathcal{E}_{\phi}[\![\, \texttt{case e in} \; ... \; \texttt{c}_k \; \texttt{x}_k \; \texttt{->} \; \texttt{e}_k \; ... \; \texttt{end} \,]\!]_{\{x \mapsto \gamma v\}}$$

which completes the proof.   □

Lemma 4.2
If γ is a projection (of the appropriate type) then $(f^{\#} \; \gamma) \circ f \sqsubseteq f \circ \gamma$

Proof
The proof is by fixed point induction. We write f_n for the nth approximation to f (that is, for $\phi_n[\![\, f \,]\!]$ where the $\{\phi_n\}$ form the Kleene chain approximating the full function environment ϕ). Recall that while f is defined by least fixed point (and so its Kleene chain of approximations is increasing), $f^{\#}$ is defined using greatest fixed point. If we define $f^{\#}_n = \phi^{\#}_n[\![\, f \,]\!]$, then $f^{\#}_0 = \lambda\gamma.ID$ and $f^{\#} \sqsubseteq f^{\#}_k$ for any integer k. We use this latter fact in the inductive case. Suppose the definition of f is given by $\texttt{f x = e}$. The induction hypothesis is that $f^{\#} \; \gamma \circ f_n \sqsubseteq f_n \circ \gamma$ for all functions f.

Case: Base

$$
\begin{aligned}
(f^{\#} \; \gamma) \circ f_0 \; &= \; (f^{\#} \; \gamma) \circ \lambda x.\bot \\
&= \; \lambda x.\bot \qquad\qquad [f^{\#} \; \gamma \; \text{is strict}] \\
&= \; f_0 \circ \gamma
\end{aligned}
$$

Case: Inductive

$$
\begin{aligned}
(f^{\#} \; \gamma) \circ f_{n+1} \; &\sqsubseteq \; (f^{\#}_{n+1} \; \gamma) \circ f_{n+1} \\
&= \; \mathcal{E}^{\#}_{\phi^{\#}_n}[\![\, e \,]\!]_{\{x \mapsto \gamma\}} \circ \lambda v.\mathcal{E}_{\phi_n}[\![\, e \,]\!]_{\{x \mapsto v\}} \\
&\sqsubseteq \; \lambda v.\mathcal{E}_{\phi_n}[\![\, e \,]\!]_{\{x \mapsto \gamma v\}} \qquad [\text{induction and lemma 4.2}] \\
&= \; f_{n+1} \circ \gamma
\end{aligned}
$$

Case: Limit

$$
\begin{aligned}
(f^{\#}\ \gamma)\ \circ\ f\ &=\ \bigsqcup_{n=0}^{\infty}\ (f^{\#}\ \gamma\ \circ\ f_n) &&[\text{continuity of } f^{\#}\ \gamma]\\
&\sqsubseteq\ \bigsqcup_{n=0}^{\infty}\ (f_n\ \circ\ \gamma) &&[\text{finite induction}]\\
&=\ f\ \circ\ \gamma &&[\text{definition of } \bigsqcup]
\end{aligned}
$$

which completes the proof. $\square$

We have proved, therefore, that the abstract version of a function maps a description of f's argument into a description of its result. The same result holds at the expression level.

Corollary 4.3
If γ is a projection (of appropriate type)

$$
e^{\#}_{[\gamma/x]}\ \circ\ \lambda v.e_{[v/x]}\ \sqsubseteq\ \lambda v.e_{[v/x]}\ \circ\ \gamma
$$

Proof
This is a restatement of the first lemma. Its precondition is satisfied by the second.
$\square$

4.5   Safety

In Chapter 3 we defined what it means for a division to be safe in terms of a slightly extended version of Jones' program model. However, that model is most suited to iterative programs where the various transfer functions, the $\{f_i\}$, are just primitive operations. In recursive programs much of the meat of the computation is likely to be performed by these transfer functions, and so we need to focus on their definitions also. To do this we will give a more general definition of safety which, in the case of iterative programs, will reduce to the one in Chapter 3. PEL programs are sufficiently similar to other recursion equation languages to serve as a suitable model directly. We write f x = $\cdots$(g e)$\cdots$ to mean that the function g appears in the definition of f with argument e (which will typically depend on x). In Jones' model the static projection σ is subscripted with the program point. For PEL programs it is subscripted with the function name—there is one static projection per function. Note that the static projection is a description of the *argument* to the function and not of the result.

Definition
Let p be a PEL program and $\Delta = (\sigma, \delta, \pi)$ be a division. Δ is safe for p if for every definition of the form f x = $\cdots$(g e)$\cdots$ in p,

$$\sigma_g \circ (\lambda v. e_{[v/x]}) = \sigma_g \circ (\lambda v. e_{[v/x]}) \circ \sigma_f$$

Writing this out fully and applying both sides to v gives the equivalent statement,

$$\sigma_g \left(\mathcal{E}_\phi [\![\, e \,]\!]_{\{x \mapsto v\}} \right) = \sigma_g \left(\mathcal{E}_\phi [\![\, e \,]\!]_{\{x \mapsto \sigma_f v\}} \right)$$

In other words, in order to calculate σ_g's worth of the argument to g we only need σ_f's worth of the argument to f.

4.6   Binding Time Analysis Equations

The abstract semantics form the basis of binding-time analysis. We want to produce a division for the program and will use the abstract semantics to do so. We introduce one more semantic domain to model program divisions. In the next chapter we will see that the functions δ_f and π_f can be derived from the static function σ_f. Therefore, all we need to model divisions is a function from variable names to static projections. Thus,

$$\Delta \quad \in \quad Divis \quad = \quad Fun \quad \rightarrow \quad Proj$$

Three functions are used to generate divisions. The function $\mathcal{P}^\#$ (corresponding to Sestoft's function P [Ses86]) produces a partial description, detailing which projections should be associated with the functions appearing in its expression argument. The other two combine this information at the program level. The value of $\mathcal{M}^\#$ is bounded by the term $\mathcal{P}^\#_{\phi\#} [\![\, e \,]\!]_{\{\lambda x.ABS\}}$ (where e is the final expression in the program) which associates the projection ABS with any free variables appearing in e.

$$\mathcal{M}^\# \; : \; Prog \; \rightarrow \; Divis$$
$$\mathcal{M}^\# [\![\, d_1, \ldots, d_n, e \,]\!] \;\; = \;\; gfp \, (\lambda \Delta \, . \, (\textstyle\bigsqcap_i \mathcal{F}^\#_{\phi\#} [\![\, d_i \,]\!]_\Delta) \sqcap \mathcal{P}^\#_{\phi\#} [\![\, e \,]\!]_{\{\lambda x.ABS\}})$$
$$\text{where}$$
$$\phi^\# \;\; = \;\; \mathcal{D}^\# [\![\, d_1, \ldots, d_n \,]\!]$$

$$\mathcal{F}^{\#} : AbsFenv \rightarrow Fndef \rightarrow Divis \rightarrow Divis$$
$$\mathcal{F}^{\#}_{\phi\#}[\![\,f\ x=e\,]\!]_{\Delta} = \mathcal{P}^{\#}_{\phi\#}[\![\,e\,]\!]_{\{x\mapsto\Delta[\![f]\!]\}}$$

$$\mathcal{P}^{\#} : AbsFenv \rightarrow Expr \rightarrow AbsVenv \rightarrow Divis$$
$$\mathcal{P}^{\#}_{\phi\#}[\![\,x\,]\!]_{\rho\#} = \{\,\lambda f\,.\,ID\,\}$$
$$\mathcal{P}^{\#}_{\phi\#}[\![\,(e_1,\ldots,e_n)\,]\!]_{\rho\#} = \mathcal{P}^{\#}_{\phi\#}[\![\,e_1\,]\!]_{\rho\#} \sqcap \ldots \sqcap \mathcal{P}^{\#}_{\phi\#}[\![\,e_n\,]\!]_{\rho\#}$$
$$\mathcal{P}^{\#}_{\phi\#}[\![\,c\ e\,]\!]_{\rho\#} = \mathcal{P}^{\#}_{\phi\#}[\![\,e\,]\!]_{\rho\#}$$
$$\mathcal{P}^{\#}_{\phi\#}[\![\,f\ e\,]\!]_{\rho\#} = \{\,f\mapsto\mathcal{E}^{\#}_{\phi\#}[\![\,e\,]\!]_{\rho\#}\,\} \sqcap \mathcal{P}^{\#}_{\phi\#}[\![\,e\,]\!]_{\rho\#}$$
$$\mathcal{P}^{\#}_{\phi\#}[\![\,\texttt{case}\ e\ \texttt{in}\ c_1\ x_1\ \texttt{->}\ e_1\ |\!|\ \ldots\ |\!|\ c_n\ x_n\ \texttt{->}\ e_n\ \texttt{end}\,]\!]_{\rho\#}$$
$$= case\ \mathcal{E}^{\#}_{\phi\#}[\![\,e\,]\!]_{\rho\#}\ in$$
$$\textstyle\sum_i c_i\ \gamma_i\ \Rightarrow\ \mathcal{P}^{\#}_{\phi\#}[\![\,e\,]\!]_{\rho\#} \sqcap (\sqcap_i\ \mathcal{P}^{\#}_{\phi\#}[\![\,e_i\,]\!]_{\rho\#\oplus\{x_i\mapsto\gamma_i\}})$$
$$else\ \ \Rightarrow\ \mathcal{P}^{\#}_{\phi\#}[\![\,e\,]\!]_{\rho\#} \sqcap (\sqcap_i\ \mathcal{P}^{\#}_{\phi\#}[\![\,e_i\,]\!]_{\rho\#\oplus\{x_i\mapsto ABS\}})$$

We will continue to use the notation σ_f for $\Delta[\![\,f\,]\!]$ when Δ is the division defined by $\mathcal{M}^{\#}$.

To show that these binding-time equations are correct we prove the following theorem.

Theorem 4.4
If p is a PEL program, the division Δ defined by $\mathcal{M}^{\#}[\![\,p\,]\!]$ is safe for p.

Proof
Suppose $f\ x = \cdots(g\ e)\cdots$ is a definition occurring in p. Then,

$$\Delta[\![\,g\,]\!] \sqsubseteq (\mathcal{F}^{\#}_{\phi\#}[\![\,f\ x = \cdots(g\ e)\cdots\,]\!]_{\Delta})\,[\![\,g\,]\!] \quad \text{[definition of } \mathcal{M}^{\#}]$$
$$= (\mathcal{P}^{\#}_{\phi\#}[\![\,\cdots(g\ e)\cdots\,]\!]_{\{x\mapsto\Delta[\![f]\!]\}})\,[\![\,g\,]\!]$$
$$\sqsubseteq (\{g\mapsto\mathcal{E}^{\#}_{\phi\#}[\![\,e\,]\!]_{\{x\mapsto\Delta[\![f]\!]\}}\})\,[\![\,g\,]\!]$$
$$= \mathcal{E}^{\#}_{\phi\#}[\![\,e\,]\!]_{\{x\mapsto\Delta[\![f]\!]\}}$$

Rewriting this in the abbreviated form gives, $\sigma_g \sqsubseteq e^{\#}_{[\sigma_f/x]}$. But, using this, we obtain

$$\sigma_g\ \circ\ \lambda v.e_{[v/x]} \sqsubseteq e^{\#}_{[\sigma_f/x]}\ \circ\ \lambda v.e_{[v/x]}$$
$$\sqsubseteq \lambda v.e_{[v/x]}\ \circ\ \sigma_f \quad \text{[corollary 4.4]}$$

which is equivalent to the safety requirement. $\quad\square$

4.7   Generating Finite Domains

The domain $Proj_X$ contains all finitary projections over X; in general, uncountably many of them. Finding the greatest fixed point required by the definition of $\mathcal{D}^\#$ is therefore uncomputable. Instead we will restrict ourselves to a finite sub-domain of projections ($FinProj_X$) and compute an approximation to the fixed point by finite iteration.

An alternative approach would be to use the infinite domain of projections. To achieve a finite analysis time, we would rely on algebraic manipulation techniques to approximate a solution to the abstract semantics equations. Hughes used this approach for backwards analysis [Hug87] and came across two problems: the algebra was complicated and tedious and, more seriously, apparently reasonable approximation methods could yield very poor results. As the use of finite domains has been successful in many areas we will adopt it here.

4.7.1   Projections

We give an explicit construction of $FinProj_X$ based on the form of the type definition defining X. In addition to projection sum and product, we define projections recursively using the fixed point operator μ. The projection $\mu\gamma.P(\gamma)$ is defined to be $\bigsqcup_{k=0}^{\infty} P^k(ABS)$ as usual (i.e. the least fixed point). In order to cope with mutual recursion we ought also to define a selection operator, but as this obscures rather than clarifies the material we will omit it here. An equivalent technique appears in the implementation.

Each finite domain $FinProj_X$ is defined by the inference rules below. A projection γ is in $FinProj_X$ if γ **proj** X can be inferred using these rules.

$$ABS \textbf{ proj } c_1\ T_1 + \cdots + c_n\ T_n$$

$$\frac{P_1 \textbf{ proj } T_1 \quad \cdots \quad P_n \textbf{ proj } T_n}{c_1\ P_1 + \cdots + c_n\ P_n \quad \textbf{proj} \quad c_1\ T_1 + \cdots + c_n\ T_n}$$

$$\frac{P_1 \text{ proj } T_1 \quad \cdots \quad P_n \text{ proj } T_n}{P_1 \times \cdots \times P_n \quad \text{proj} \quad (T_1, \ldots, T_n)}$$

$$\frac{P(\gamma) \text{ proj } T(t) \quad [\gamma \text{ proj } t]}{\mu\gamma.P(\gamma) \text{ proj } \mu t.T(t)}$$

The final rule should be read, "if $P(\gamma)$ **proj** $T(t)$ can be inferred under the assumption that γ **proj** t then $\mu\gamma.P(\gamma)$ **proj** $\mu t.T(t)$ can be inferred."

Because type definitions are finite, it is easy to see that if any type X is defined using the base types and $+$, $\times$ and μ then $FinProj_X$ is a finite domain.

Which projections are included in $FinProj_X$? Certainly ABS always is (possibly occurring as $ABS \times ABS$ or $\mu\gamma.ABS$). ID also is always included, though this may not be immediately obvious, particularly in the recursive case. However, if $P(\gamma)$ **proj** $T(t)$ (under the assumption that γ **proj** t) and if $P(ID_t) = ID_{T(t)}$, then $\mu\gamma.P(\gamma) = ID_{\mu t.T(t)}$ as required. Over a product domain we have only those projections which act on the components separately. If X is a sum domain then $FinProj_X$ contains the ABS projection and, in addition, projections which discriminate between all the injective tags. The only projections we have over recursive domains are those which treat every level of recursion identically. Finally, we note that $ABS_1 = ID_1$ as there is only one projection on the one point domain.

4.7.2 Examples

To make this clearer, we will consider the following examples. Suppose that for some types X and Y, $FinProj_X = \{ABS, ID\} = FinProj_Y$. Then the elements of $FinProj_{(X,Y)}$ are given by

$$\begin{aligned} FinProj_{(X,Y)} &= \{ABS \times ABS, \; ID \times ABS, \; ABS \times ID, \; ID \times ID\} \\ &= \{ABS, \; LEFT, \; RIGHT, \; ID\} \end{aligned}$$

To take another example, suppose that the type Union is a tagged union of Bool, Int, and Char. That is,

```
type Union = Bl Bool + Num Int + Ch Char
```

The elements of $FinProj_{Union}$ are ABS, TAG (which retains the tag but discards everything else), ID, and six projections lying between TAG and ID which variously discard values in one or two of the summed domains (under the assumption that the projections over these types are just ABS and ID). This means that, not only can we model total presence or absence of information, but we can also model partial information—knowing only the tag but not the associated value for example. If we have a function that operates on a tagged union our partial evaluator may, at least potentially, be able to evaluate away the tags to provide separate functions specialised to arguments of the different types. This is a key idea in the development in the next chapter.

Finally, consider association lists as used to implement environments. Assuming we have two other types `Var` and `Val` we could define,

```
type Assoc = End + More ((Var, Val), Assoc)
```

The projections in $FinProj_{Assoc}$ include ABS and ID as usual. In addition we have $STRUCT$ (where only the recursive structure is known) and $STRUCT(LEFT)$ and $STRUCT(RIGHT)$ which discard the `Val` are `Var` parts respectively. These are ordered as follows.

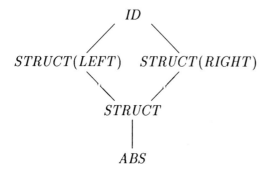

Using these projections, we can model the situation where we know only the names in an environment but not the values, for example. This situation is likely to occur during partial evaluation of an interpreter. It means that it should not be necessary to write interpreters with separate name and value lists in order to benefit from partial evaluation.

4.7.3   Relating to $Proj_X$

We must relate the domains $FinProj_X$ and $Proj_X$. The inclusion map supplies a suitable embedding of $FinProj_X$ in $Proj_X$. The corresponding projection from $Proj_X$ to $FinProj_X$ is given by,

$$fold\ \gamma = max\ \{\beta \in FinProj_X \mid \beta \sqsubseteq \gamma\}$$

Currently, the abstract semantics are defined over the whole of $Proj$. By applying $fold$ to every right hand side in $\mathcal{E}^{\#}$, we obtain an approximation to the abstract semantics whose values are all in the appropriate finite domains of projections. (Actually, because of the construction of the finite domains, $fold$ only needs to be applied in the constructor case). As $fold$ is a projection (on projections—see Chapter 6, Section 2.1), the finite abstract semantics underestimate the true abstract semantics, so the proof of safety still holds.

4.8   Summary

After defining a small typed language together with its concrete semantics, we defined an alternative semantics that manipulates projections. These alternative semantics were shown to abstract the notion of static data correctly with respect to the concrete semantics. Consequently, we were able to show that the equations intended to produce a congruent division were also correct. Finally, we demonstrated how to approximate the abstract semantics in a safe and computationally feasible way.

We now know how to describe the static data. In the next chapter we turn our attention to the dynamic.

Chapter 5

Run Time Arguments

The static projection tells us which part of a function's argument will be present during partial evaluation. In any particular call of the function, this part of the argument is used in the production of a residual function. However, this still leaves the question: which part of the argument should the residual function be given at run-time? Obviously we could pass the whole argument if we wanted to, but we can do a lot better. After all, we assume that the partial evaluator will have taken the static part of the argument into account in producing the residual function. It ought to be unnecessary to supply the residual function with the same information all over again.

We need a way to select the run-time information. The original argument to a function f must be factorised, or decomposed, into static and dynamic factors, and this factorisation should be as complete as possible. That is, the amount of static information which is also regarded as dynamic should be minimised. Then, when we pass the dynamic argument to the residual function, we will be passing as little information at run-time as possible. There are, of course, many possible factorisation methods. Some produce an exact decomposition while others do not in that they contain extra junk.

We will look at two methods in this chapter. While the first does not produce an exact factorisation of the original argument, it is based on very familiar constructions and is interesting in its own right. The second method, which is exact, arises as a generalisation of the first, and provides a practical application of some fairly deep mathematics.

5.1 Projection Complements

The canonical equation for *mix* assumes that the program argument is defined on a product of the static and dynamic domains. So if $f : X \to Y$ is a function defined in the program, we would like to regard it as having the type $f : A \times B \to Y$, where A is static and B dynamic. Assuming we are supplied with a static projection γ for f we can produce A—it is just isomorphic to the range of the static projection, which we write as $\gamma(\!(X)\!)$ (this is a domain as all the elements of each $FinProj_X$ are finitary projections). Ideally, we would like to pick another projection, δ say, so that $B = \delta(\!(X)\!)$ and $X \cong A \times B$, exactly factorising X. Unfortunately, this is not possible in general, as even an optimum choice of δ may define a domain B which is too large. However, while we cannot achieve isomorphism we can ensure that, in some sense, X is a sub-domain of $A \times B$. A trivial solution to this is for δ to be the identity function and then B would equal X. Fortunately we can do better.

Suppose we are given a static projection and want the dynamic function to be a projection also. This dynamic projection must be a *complement* of the static.

Definition
If $\gamma : D \to D$ and $\beta : D \to D$ are projections, and if $\gamma \sqcup \beta = ID$, then β is a *complement* of γ (and vice versa).

There may be many projections which are complements of a projection γ. We will choose one in particular and describe it as *the* complement of γ, written $\overline{\gamma}$.

From the definition it is clear that for each value $x \in D$ the property that $\gamma x \sqcup \overline{\gamma} x = x$ holds. In other words, between a projection and its complement no information is lost. But for it to be a good choice, the complement should discard as much as possible consistent with this. That is, the complement should be as small as possible. In general there is no least complement, but as we are only interested in static projections drawn from an appropriate $FinProj_D$ we will take its complement from there also. If we do this then we can choose one which is minimal.

We know that D can be embedded in $\sigma(\!(D)\!) \times \delta(\!(D)\!)$ when σ and δ are complements because the canonical map $< \sigma, \delta > : D \to \sigma(\!(D)\!) \times \delta(\!(D)\!)$ is injective. That is, if $(\sigma\ d,\ \delta\ d) = (\sigma\ d',\ \delta\ d')$ for $d, d' \in D$ then $d = \sigma\ d \sqcup \delta\ d = \sigma\ d' \sqcup \delta\ d' = d'$.

5.1.1   Constructing Complements

In the previous chapter, elements of *FinProj$_X$* were defined constructively. For any such projection, we can give a corresponding construction of its complement.

$$\overline{ABS} \qquad\qquad\qquad = \quad ID$$

$$\overline{ID} \qquad\qquad\qquad = \quad ABS$$

$$\overline{c_1\ \gamma_1 + \cdots + c_n\ \gamma_n} \quad = \quad c_1\ \overline{\gamma}_1 + \cdots + c_n\ \overline{\gamma}_n \quad \text{if } \gamma_i \neq ID \text{ for some } i$$

$$\overline{\gamma_1 \times \cdots \times \gamma_n} \qquad = \quad \overline{\gamma}_1 \times \cdots \times \overline{\gamma}_n$$

$$\overline{\mu\gamma.P(\gamma)} \qquad\qquad = \quad \mu\gamma.\overline{P}(\gamma)$$

Note that the case where $\gamma_i = ID$ is covered by $\overline{ID} = ABS$.

It is not hard to establish that $\gamma \sqcup \overline{\gamma} = ID$ for all $\gamma \in Proj_D$. The only non-trivial case is the recursive one. This may be established by recognising that $\overline{P^n(\gamma)} = \overline{P}^n(\overline{\gamma})$ for all n and that $ABS_1 = ID_1$ on the one point domain. As $\mu t.\,T(t) = \bigsqcup_{k=0}^{\infty} T^k(1)$ we can appeal to continuity to complete the result. The details may be found in [Lau88].

An example will show that the factorisation is not always exact. Suppose that D is the `Assoc` domain from the previous chapter—essentially a list of pairs—and that the static projection is $STRUCT$ which discards all the elements leaving only the list structure. What is the complement of $STRUCT$? If we restrict ourselves to elements of $Proj_D$ then the answer is ID. As $STRUCT(\!(Assoc)\!) \cong List_1$ (lists of elements of the void type) it is clear that $Assoc \not\cong STRUCT(\!(Assoc)\!) \times Assoc$. This example also shows that the complement of the complement of a projection is not necessarily equal to the original projection itself.

5.1.2   Examples

What sort of residual functions are produced when we use complements? Some examples will be useful.

The simplest case is where the argument to a function is a tuple of values each of which is either completely static or completely dynamic. Here projections provide exactly the same results as the original DIKU work.

A more challenging, but now standard, example is given by the association lists described in the previous chapter. Suppose we have the function `lookup` which takes an association list and an index value and returns the value associated with the index. Thus,

```
lookup :: (Assoc,Var) -> Val;
lookup (xys,w)
  = case xys in
        Empty                => fail
     || More ((x,y),xys') => case equal (x,w) in
                                   False => lookup (xys',w)
                                || True  => y
                              end;
     end;
```

where `fail` and `equal` are suitably defined. The association list associates variable names with values. Suppose that we know the names at specialise-time but not the values, as we might when specialising an interpreter to a program, for example. Each call to the function `lookup` in the original program will be replaced by calls to specialised versions of it. The static projection for `lookup` will be $\sigma : (Assoc \times Var) \rightarrow (Assoc \times Var)$ given by $\sigma (a, v) = (STRUCT(LEFT)\ a,\ v)$. Its complement is given by $\delta (a, v) = (STRUCT(RIGHT)\ a,\ \perp)$. Thus the parameter to the residual function will be from a domain isomorphic to the range of the dynamic projection δ—essentially a list of values. The specialised versions of `lookup` will move down this list of values a set distance, and return the value found there. So, not only is there no testing on the names in the environment at run-time, but the names have totally vanished. Knowing this, we could rewrite the the example in Chapter 2 so that the state is modelled by a single association list without affecting the results of partial evaluation.

A less successful result occurs with the `Union` type. If the static projection is *TAG* then the dynamic projection is *ID*. So, although a function body using a value of the `Union` type may be streamlined somewhat to its argument, the whole argument is still used at run-time—the value is still packaged up with its tag. The consequent packaging and unpackaging constitutes an unnecessary inefficiency. While not too serious in this example, it is symptomatic of the weakness of the complement method.

5.2   Program Divisions

Using complementary projections to factorise the argument to a function into its static and dynamic components is an example of a *program division* [Jon88]. We have already touched on this informally in Chapter 3, but will now give its precise definition. It is cast in terms of Jones' program model.

Definition   (Jones)
A *program division* is a triple (σ, δ, π) where $\sigma_p : V \rightarrow V_s$, $\delta_p : V \rightarrow V_d$, and $\pi_p : V_s \times V_d \rightarrow V$ for each program point p, such that for all $v \in V$, $v_s \in V_s$, and $v_d \in V_d$,

$$
\begin{array}{lll}
\text{(i)} & \pi_p\left(\sigma_p\ v,\ \delta_p\ v\right) & = & v \\
\text{(ii)} & \sigma_p\left(\pi_p\left(v_s, v_d\right)\right) & = & v_s \\
\text{(iii)} & \delta_p\left(\pi_p\left(v_s, v_d\right)\right) & = & v_d
\end{array}
$$

The first condition requires that between them, the static and dynamic functions do not lose any information—the pairing function π_p is able to reconstitute the original value from the two parts. The other two conditions imply that the static parts stay static, and the dynamic dynamic.

This intuition is very similar to the informal justification we offered for using complementary projections. There is a good reason for this. Suppose we were to choose V_s and V_d to be sub-domains of the original domain, and the pairing function π_p to be least upper bound. Then for the static and dynamic functions to form a division, they must be complementary projections. Why projections? Because, for example, condition (i) requires that $(\sigma_p\ v) \sqcup (\delta_p\ v) = v$ for all values v, which implies that $\sigma_p \sqsubseteq ID$. In addition, condition (ii) requires that $\sigma_p\left(v_s \sqcup v_d\right) = v_s$ for all values v_s and v_d. Choosing $v_d = \bot$ and expressing v_s as $(\sigma_p\ v)$ for some value v gives $\sigma_p\left(\sigma_p\ v\right) = \sigma_p\ v$. Thus, σ_p is idempotent and weaker that ID. It is a projection. Exactly the same argument applies to δ. Why must they be complements? Condition (i), when expressed using least upper bound for π_p, is precisely the complement condition.

We can extend this slightly. Rather than insist that V_s and V_d are *actually* sub-domains of V it is sufficient for them to be isomorphic to sub-domains. It then still makes sense to talk of the least upper bound of elements drawn from V_s and V_d.

From all this we draw the conclusion: If the pairing function π from a division is essentially least upper bound, then the static and dynamic functions σ and δ are essentially complementary domain projections.

There are other choices for the pairing function which give rise to different sorts of divisions. In the previous section we pointed out some of the shortcomings of the complement division. We will now study a more complicated division, but one which provides an exact factorisation.

5.3 Domain-Theoretic Dependent Sum

In the introduction to the chapter, we noted that it is usually impossible to find non-trivial factorisations of an arbitrary domain X as the product of two others. The problem is that the domain product operation is too restrictive. We need some more general operation from which product arises as a special case. That more general operation is *dependent sum*.

Dependent sum is usually thought of as a set construction and is often associated with constructive type (set) theory [Mar80] where it occurs as a primitive. However, in its domain form it made its debut in an exercise in Plotkin's lecture notes in 1978 [Plo78]. Since then it has been used to provide models for the polymorphic λ-calculus [CGW87]. Categorically speaking, dependent sum is a Grothendieck construction where the underlying domain is viewed as a category. This aspect is particularly relevant later on.

In order to develop a basic understanding we will give a set theoretic definition of dependent sum, and then show how to extend it to domains.

Definition
Let A be a set and $\{B_a\}$ a family of sets indexed by elements of A. Then the *dependent sum* $\sum_{a \in A} B_a$ is the set,

$$\sum_{a \in A} B_a = \{(a, b) \mid a \in A, \ b \in B_a\}$$

The dependent sum is a (possibly infinite) tagged union of the family of sets $\{B_a\}$. If the family is constant, i.e. if there exists some set B such that $B_a = B$ for every $a \in A$ then $\sum_{a \in A} B_a$ reduces to the set product $A \times B$.

Now suppose that A and the family $\{B_a\}_{a \in A}$ are domains and not just sets. Let us consider what it means to index a family of domains by a domain. It is clear what it means to index by a set, but a domain has more structure and this should be taken into account. We might quite reasonably require that as we move up a chain in the indexing domain, the corresponding domains in the family become larger. That is, if $a, a' \in A$ are indexing elements such that $a \sqsubseteq a'$ then there must be an embedding $\phi_{a,a'} : B_a \to B_{a'}$ which embeds B_a into $B_{a'}$. Of course, the embeddings should be such that if $a \sqsubseteq a' \sqsubseteq a''$ then $\phi_{a,a''} = \phi_{a',a''} \circ \phi_{a,a'}$. This much reflects the ordering relation on the domain. We must also express completeness. If we have a directed set $V \subseteq A$ then we require that $B_{\bigsqcup V} = \bigsqcup \{B_a \mid a \in V\}$ and that for any $a \sqsubseteq \bigsqcup V$ the embedding $\phi_{a, \bigsqcup V}$ is given by $\phi_{a, \bigsqcup V} = \bigsqcup \{\phi_{a,a'} \mid a' \in V\}$ (we use the least upper bound of domains following Scott's information systems; in some other framework it may be replaced by colimit or union, for example).

This may be expressed very concisely categorically. First, we may view the indexing domain as a category: the domain elements are the objects of the category, and there is a single arrow from one object to another exactly when the first approximates the second in the domain ordering. Transitivity and reflexivity of the ordering provide composition and the identity arrows respectively. Secondly, domains together with embedding/projection pairs (that is, pairs of functions $\phi : X \to Y$, $\psi : Y \to X$ such that $\psi \circ \phi = id_X$ and $\phi \circ \psi \sqsubseteq id_Y$) form a category, which we shall denote as Dom^{ep}. Given these facts, a domain-indexed family of domains corresponds precisely to a continuous functor from the index domain to Dom^{ep}.

Now that we know what a domain-indexed family of domains is, we can construct the dependent sum.

Definition   (Domain Dependent Sum)
If $\{B_a\}_{a \in A}$ is a domain-indexed family of domains, then the *dependent sum* of the family is given by,

$$\sum_{a \in A} B_a = \{(a, b) \mid a \in A, \ b \in B_a\}$$

with the ordering

$$(a, b) \sqsubseteq_\Sigma (a', b') \Leftrightarrow (a \sqsubseteq_A a') \wedge (\phi_{a,a'}(b) \sqsubseteq_{B_{a'}} b')$$

Lemma 5.1

The dependent sum of a domain-indexed family of domains is a domain.

Sketch Proof

A complete proof that this construction results in a Scott domain appears in [CGW87] but we will give an outline here. We need to show that the sum is an ω-algebraic, consistently complete, complete partial order. It is clear that it has a bottom element, given by $(\perp_A, \perp_{B_{\perp_A}})$, and the fact that the relation $\sqsubseteq$ over the elements of the sum is a partial order follows almost immediately from the fact that $\sqsubseteq_A$ and the $\sqsubseteq_{B_a}$ are all partial orders.

To construct the least upper bound of a directed set of elements drawn from the sum we initially consider the set of first components. These form a directed set in A which will have a least upper bound. If all the second components of the original directed set are injected into the domain indexed by this least upper bound, then again we obtain a directed set which will itself have a least upper bound. The pair, whose components are the two least upper bounds, is an element of the dependent sum and is the least upper bound of the original set. We can form the least upper bound of a consistent set in the same way.

To show algebraicity we have to characterise the finite elements. An element (a, b) of the sum is finite exactly when a is finite in A and b is finite in B_a. The set of finite approximations to an element form a directed set. Because A and the $\{B_a\}$ are algebraic, and because the indexing is continuous, the least upper bound of this directed set will be the original element. Finally, because A and the $\{B_a\}$ have countable bases, the set of finite elements is countable. $\square$

As we might expect, domain product is a special case of domain dependent sum. To see this suppose that $B_a = B$ for every $a \in A$. The elements of the sum are then just the elements of the product. Furthermore, all the embeddings are constrained to be the identity, and so the order relation simplifies to the usual product ordering.

We have retained the set style notation for dependent sum even though it does not make the embeddings explicit. To be fully formal we should work with the functors given by the categorical view. Later on, when we do need the formality, we will do this. Elsewhere, however, we will use the set notation in the belief that familiar notation is helpful.

5.4   Projection Factorisation

Let us summarise what we have done. We started with a domain-indexed family of domains. From this, we produced a sum domain that respects the structure of the indexing domain. In this section we do things the other way around. We start off with a single domain and discover a domain-indexed family of domains sitting inside it. This allow us to express the original domain as a dependent sum.

We have already noted that domain-theoretic dependent sum is a special case of the (covariant) Grothendieck construction. This (very general) construction has a corresponding decomposition, namely the Grothendieck cofibration. Cofibrations have the property that they give rise to an indexed family whose Grothendieck construction reconstructs the original structure. It turns out that cofibration is precisely the concept we require in order to generalise our earlier notions of projection complements.

Consider a call of some function, $(f\ x)$ say, and suppose that γ is the static projection for f. During partial evaluation, we will be able to compute the static portion of x using γ. Call this value a. Hence $a = \gamma\ x$. At partial evaluation time, the value a represents the sum total of our knowledge about the value x. Prior to calculating the static value, all we would have known about x was its type, X say. Now, however, we can be more precise. Not only must x lie in X, but it must also lie in the inverse image of a under γ. That is, $x \in \gamma^{-1}\{a\}$. This might provide fairly tight constraints on the possible value of x. How tight the constraints are will depend on γ, of course. If γ is a large projection (indicating lots of static information) its inverse images (or *fibres*) will be relatively small but, conversely, if γ is small (not much static information) its fibres will be large.

A question naturally arises. Given that the fibres are subsets of the domain, what sort of structure do they have? We shall prove that for the projections we use, not only are all the fibres Scott domains, but they also correspond to first-order constructible types. In particular, they are just products of types that already appear within the source program.

With these observations our overall strategy should have become clear. The range of the static projection forms a domain which indexes the family of its fibres, each of these being domains. It should, therefore, be possible to express the original domain as a dependent sum, where each of the summands is the inverse image of some static value. In any particular function application, we will know that the dynamic value must be constrained to the fibre corresponding to the static value, and so may express the type of the residual function accordingly.

Towards the end of the chapter we will see some examples of this in practice, but in the meantime will show that the strategy may be realised.

5.4.1   Cofibration

When is a projection a cofibration? That is, when does it give rise to a family of domains whose dependent sum is isomorphic to the original domain? Rather than give a very general answer we will show that the projections we use do indeed have this property. Unsurprisingly, we induct over the projection constructions. This approach is sufficiently flexible so that if another domain construction were added at any time then it alone would need to be checked.

For the present we will take on trust that all the fibres form domains. We will present a lemma shortly which gives the stronger result mentioned previously. Our immediate task is to demonstrate that appropriate embeddings exist.

Definition
Let $\gamma : X \to X$ be a projection in $FinProj_X$ (Section 4.7) with $x, x' \in \gamma(\!(X)\!)$ such that $x \sqsubseteq x'$. Then $\widehat{\gamma}_{x,x'} : \gamma^{-1}\{x\} \to \gamma^{-1}\{x'\}$ is a mapping from $\gamma^{-1}\{x\}$ into $\gamma^{-1}\{x'\}$ where the $\widehat{}$ operation is defined inductively by

$$\widehat{\gamma \times \delta}_{(x,y),\,(x',y')} \;=\; \widehat{\gamma}_{x,x'} \,\times\, \widehat{\delta}_{y,y'}$$

$$\widehat{ABS}_{\perp,\perp} \qquad\quad =\; id$$

$$\widehat{\gamma + \delta}_{\perp,\;inl\;x'} \quad =\; \lambda x.x' \qquad\qquad \text{(likewise for } inr\text{)}$$

$$\widehat{\gamma + \delta}_{inl\;x,\;inl\;x'} \;=\; \widehat{\gamma}_{x,x'} \,+\, id \qquad \text{(likewise for } inr\text{)}$$

$$\widehat{\mu\gamma.P(\gamma)}_{x,x'} \quad =\; \bigsqcup\nolimits_n \,(\phi_n \circ P^n(\widehat{ABS}))_{\psi_n x,\,\psi_n x'} \circ \psi_n)$$

where $(\phi_n, \psi_n) : T^n(\perp) \to \mu t.T(t)$ is the canonical embedding/projection pair.

Lemma 5.2

Let $\gamma : X \to X$ be a projection in $FinProj_X$ with $x, x' \in \gamma(\!(X)\!)$ such that $x \sqsubseteq x'$. Then $\hat{\gamma}_{x,x'} : \gamma^{-1}\{x\} \to \gamma^{-1}\{x'\}$ is an embedding with the property that

$$a \sqsubseteq a' \;\Leftrightarrow\; \hat{\gamma}_{x,x'}(a) \sqsubseteq a'$$

for any $a \in \gamma^{-1}\{x\}$ and $a' \in \gamma^{-1}\{x'\}$.

Proof

The only case in which the result is not immediately obvious is the recursive case. To simplify notation we will write P^n for $P^n(ABS)$ and P^ω for $\mu\gamma.P(\gamma)$. We need to show three things. Firstly that $\widehat{P^\omega}_{x,x'}$ does indeed map elements of the x fibre to elements of the x' fibre. Secondly that the map is an embedding, and finally that it preserves order.

Let a be an element in the x fibre (that is, $P^\omega\, a = x$). In order to show that $\widehat{P^\omega}_{x,x'}$ maps elements of the x fibre into the x' fibre, we must show that $P^\omega\left(\widehat{P^\omega}_{x,x'}\, a\right) = x'$.

$$
\begin{aligned}
&\left(P^\omega \circ \widehat{P^\omega}_{x,x'}\right)(a) \\
&= \left(P^\omega \circ \left(\bigsqcup_n \phi_n \circ \widehat{P^n}_{\psi_n x,\ \psi_n x'} \circ \psi_n\right)\right)(a) && [\text{defn of } \widehat{P^\omega}] \\
&= \left(\bigsqcup_n P^\omega \circ \phi_n \circ \widehat{P^n}_{\psi_n x,\ \psi_n x'} \circ \psi_n\right)(a) && [\text{continuity}] \\
&= \left(\bigsqcup_n \bigsqcup_k \phi_k \circ P^k \circ \psi_k \circ \phi_n \circ \widehat{P^n}_{\psi_n x,\ \psi_n x'} \circ \psi_n\right)(a) && [\text{defn of } P^\omega] \\
&= \left(\bigsqcup_n \phi_n \circ P^n \circ \psi_n \circ \phi_n \circ \widehat{P^n}_{\psi_n x,\ \psi_n x'} \circ \psi_n\right)(a) && [\text{rearranging}] \\
&= \left(\bigsqcup_n \phi_n \circ P^n \circ \widehat{P^n}_{\psi_n x,\ \psi_n x'} \circ \psi_n\right)(a) && [\psi_n \circ \phi_n = id] \\
&= \bigsqcup_n \phi_n \left(P^n \left(\widehat{P^n}_{\psi_n x,\ \psi_n x'} (\psi_n\, a)\right)\right) \\
&= \bigsqcup_n \phi_n (\psi_n\, x') && [\text{finite induction}] \\
&= x' && [\text{algebraicity}]
\end{aligned}
$$

To see that $\widehat{P^\omega}_{x,x'}$ is an embedding we only need to note that (by finite induction) its approximations are all embeddings on larger and larger subdomains. In the limit we obtain an embedding on the whole domain. Finally, suppose that $a \sqsubseteq a'$ (where $a \in \gamma^{-1}\{x\}$ and $a' \in \gamma^{-1}\{x'\}$). As order between the finite approximations of a and a' (namely, $\psi_n\, a$ and $\psi_n\, a'$) is preserved by the approximations to $\widehat{P^\omega}_{x,x'}$ (an easy induction), then order is also preserved in the limit. $\square$

We are now in a position to show that all the projections in $FinProj_X$ are cofibrations. Their fibres form an indexed family of domains such that, when we construct their dependent sum, we obtain a domain isomorphic to the original. This, our main result, is expressed in the following theorem.

Theorem 5.3 (Projection Factorisation)
If $\gamma : X \to X$ is an element of $FinProj_X$ then

$$X \cong \sum_{a \in \gamma(X)} \gamma^{-1}\{a\}$$

Proof
The elements of the sum are all of the form $(\gamma\ x,\ x)$ and so are in one-to-one correspondence with the elements of X. Furthermore, both X and the sum have the same ordering, for

$$
\begin{aligned}
&(\gamma\ x,\ x) \sqsubseteq_\Sigma (\gamma\ x',\ x') \\
&\Leftrightarrow\ (\gamma\ x \sqsubseteq_X \gamma\ x') \wedge (\widehat{\gamma}_{\gamma x, \gamma x'}(x) \sqsubseteq_X x') &&\text{[definition]} \\
&\Leftrightarrow\ (\gamma\ x \sqsubseteq_X \gamma\ x') \wedge (x \sqsubseteq_X x') &&\text{[lemma 5.2]} \\
&\Leftrightarrow\ x \sqsubseteq_X x' &&\text{[γ monotonic]}
\end{aligned}
$$

which completes the proof. □

The factorisation theorem allows an arbitrary domain to be decomposed in many different ways depending on the choice of projection. In contrast with using projection complements, this factorisation is exact. That is, we obtain a new structure which is isomorphic to the original. The factorisation is relevant to partial evaluation because it can be driven by the projection obtained as the result of binding-time analysis. However, there is still an issue open. We must show that all the fibres form domains. We actually want something stronger than this. As the fibres correspond to the possible dynamic values we would like to produce a residual function whose argument type corresponds to the fibre. We need to know, therefore, whether the fibres are expressible in the type system. Fortunately, in most cases they are. We will consider a few examples before proving the result in general.

Consider the `Assoc` type again (Section 4.7), together with the projection $STRUCT$ that discards all the elements. The element `More ((⊥,⊥), End)` is in the range of $STRUCT$ and its inverse image is isomorphic to the domain `(Var,Val)`. Again, the element `More ((⊥,⊥), More ((⊥,⊥), End))` is also in the range of $STRUCT$.

Its inverse image is isomorphic to the domain (Var,Val,Var,Val). To take another example consider the Union type together with the projection TAG which discards everything except the injection tags. The element Num $\perp$ is in the range of TAG and its inverse image is isomorphic to Int.

These examples are typical and may be generalised to any finite element in the range of a projection, as the following theorem makes clear.

Theorem 5.4
Let X be a domain and $\sigma \in FinProj_X$ a projection. If $a \in \sigma(|X|)$ is a finite element then there exists a domain $B_a \cong \sigma^{-1}\{a\}$ such that B_a is expressible in the type system.

Sketch Proof
The proof is by induction over the static projection constructions. If the projection is ABS then the inverse image is just one of the domains we started with and so is expressible in the type system. In the sum and product cases the induction is straightforward. For the recursive case we appeal to the restriction that the static value is finite. In this case we only need to apply the recursive rule finitely often and so will end up with a finite product of domains each expressible in the type system. $\square$

The restriction in the theorem to finite elements ensures that we will never need to construct an infinite product. There is in principle no reason why we should not, except that many languages (including PEL) exclude such constructions. Nonetheless, this is not a serious restriction. Attempting to specialise a function to an infinite value will fall foul of the infinity problem, and the partial evaluator will loop. If the division is finite (Chapter 2, Section 3) then no infinite values will arise.

5.4.2   Domain Dependent Products

In order to describe the action of the partial evaluator we need to define dependent products. Again these are more familiar in set theory than domain theory, but we may define them quite easily after having defined dependent sum.

Definition   (Domain Dependent Product)
If $\{B_a\}_{a \in A}$ is a domain-indexed family of domains then the *dependent product* of the family is given by,

$$\prod_{a \in A} B_a = \{f \mid \forall a \in A \,.\, f_a \in B_a\}$$

where the elements f are continuous families indexed by A with the ordering

$$f \sqsubseteq_\Pi g \Leftrightarrow \forall a \in A.\, f_a \sqsubseteq_{B_a} g_a$$

The elements of the product are like functions except that their range is not very clearly defined. Supplying an indexing element $a \in A$ produces an element of the corresponding B_a. Each family is continuous, so if $a \sqsubseteq a'$ then $\phi_{a,a'}(f_a) \sqsubseteq_{B_a} f_{a'}$ and if $a = \bigsqcup\{a_i\}$ then $f_a = \bigsqcup\{\phi_{a_i,a}(f_{a_i})\}$.

A proof that dependent product is a Scott domain appears in [CGW87]. An equivalent formulation defines the elements of the product to be the continuous sections of the first projection from the dependent sum. That is, the elements are functions $f : A \to \sum_{a \in A} B_a$ such that $fst \circ f = id_A$. Such functions must have the form $f\, a = (a, b)$ where $b \in B_a$. This formulation makes it very clear that, if the family of domains is constant, then the dependent product $\prod_{a \in A} B$ is isomorphic to the function space $(A \to B)$.

There is an important isomorphism between function spaces from dependent sums and dependent products of function spaces.

Lemma 5.5
If $\{B_a\}_{a \in A}$ is a domain-indexed family of domains, and if C is some domain, then

$$(\sum_{a \in A} B_a) \to C \;\cong\; \prod_{a \in A} (B_a \to C)$$

Proof
This can be proved directly for the case of domains, but we can give an elegant category theoretic proof (communicated to me by Andrew Pitts). The details may be skipped without serious consequences.

The isomorphism is a consequence of the following adjoint situation. Let Dom be
the usual category of domains and continuous functions, Dom^{ep} be the category
of domains with embedding/projection pairs, and $[A \rightarrow Dom^{ep}]$ be the category of
continuous functors from the domain A (viewed as a category) to Dom^{ep}. This latter
category corresponds to domain-indexed families of domains. There is a functor
$\Delta : Dom \rightarrow [A \rightarrow Dom^{ep}]$ (called the *diagonal functor*) which maps any domain D
into the constant functor Δ_D (i.e the constant family $\{D\}_{a \in A}$). This functor has
both a left and a right adjoint which are dependent sum and product, respectively
(written $\sum \dashv \Delta \dashv \prod$). Let X be an arbitrary domain and $B : A \rightarrow Dom^{ep}$ be a functor
corresponding to an indexed family of domains $\{B_a\}_{a \in A}$. Then all the following are
natural isomorphisms:

$$
\begin{aligned}
&Hom(X,\ (\textstyle\sum B) \rightarrow C) \\
&\cong\ Hom(\textstyle\sum B,\ X \rightarrow C) &&[\text{currying twice and product commutative}] \\
&\cong\ Hom(B,\ \Delta(X \rightarrow C)) &&[\textstyle\sum \dashv \Delta] \\
&\cong\ Hom(B,\ \Delta X \rightarrow \Delta C) &&[\Delta \text{ preserves } \rightarrow] \\
&\cong\ Hom(\Delta X,\ B \rightarrow \Delta C) &&[\text{currying twice and product commutative}] \\
&\cong\ Hom(X,\ \textstyle\prod(B \rightarrow \Delta C)) &&[\Delta \dashv \textstyle\prod]
\end{aligned}
$$

Thus, $Hom(\ \_\ ,\ (\sum B) \rightarrow C)$ is naturally isomorphic to $Hom(\ \_\ ,\ \prod(B \rightarrow \Delta C))$ and
so, by the Yoneda lemma, $(\sum B) \rightarrow C \cong \prod(B \rightarrow \Delta C)$. Written in the notation of
families this is just $(\sum_{a \in A} B_a) \rightarrow C \cong \prod_{a \in A}(B_a \rightarrow C)$. $\square$

Using this isomorphism, we are able to describe the action of a partial evaluator.
Suppose we start with some function $f : X \rightarrow Y$ together with a partial description
of a value $x \in X$. Let $\gamma : X \rightarrow X$ be the static projection, so that the partial description of the value $x \in X$ gives us complete information about the value $\gamma\, x \in \gamma(\!(X)\!)$.
As the domain X is isomorphic to the domain $\sum_{a \in \gamma(\!(X)\!)}(\gamma^{-1}\{a\})$, we may view f as a
function $f : (\sum_{a \in \gamma(\!(X)\!)}(\gamma^{-1}\{a\})) \rightarrow Y$. Now, we are in a position to appeal to the isomorphism above, and so also view f as an indexed family $f \in \prod_{a \in \gamma(\!(X)\!)}(\gamma^{-1}\{a\} \rightarrow Y)$.
Supplying the index value $a = (\gamma\, x)$ gives us the corresponding residual function
$f_a : \gamma^{-1}\{a\} \rightarrow Y$.

We may interpret the isomorphism above as a statement about the existence (and
uniqueness) of the residual functions. It states that any function may be viewed as
a collection (product) of (residual) functions, one for each static value. Furthermore,
this result does not depend on the static value being in a particular form, but holds

for any projection which is also a cofibration (i.e which will allow a dependent sum construction). As we know, the purpose of binding-time analysis is to chose a projection which accurately describes the static information. We can now see *mix* as the means for extracting the appropriate residual function.

Of course, as with the S-*m*-*n* theorem, this view says nothing about the engineering aspects of *mix* (efficiency of the residual programs etc.) but only about the existence of the residual functions. It is, therefore, important to remember that a partial evaluator actually manipulates programs (i.e. representations of functions) rather than functions themselves. As such, each of the steps above require a fair amount of symbolic manipulation to achieve in practice. The description above expresses *extensionally* what happens to the functions, but says very little about the algorithms that achieve it through *intensional* manipulation.

The type of Mix

The version of *mix* that uses dependent sum has a correspondingly more general type than that appearing in Chapter 1.

$$
mix :: \overline{(\sum_{a \in A} B_a) \to C} \;\to\; \prod_{a \in A} \overline{(B_a \to C)}
$$

Providing *mix* with a function as its argument produces a dependent product, that is, an indexed family. Supplying this family with an index value (the static information) results in a residual function whose type depends on that static information. This has important consequences, as we will see in the next section.

If, in the isomorphism demonstrated above, we reduce the dependent sum and dependent product to their special cases of product and function space respectively, then the isomorphism reduces to currying. Thus, as a special case, currying remains a useful idiom for discussing partial evaluation. However, it fails to exhibit one important point: in general, the *type* of a residual function depends on the static *value* used to produce it. It is because of this fact that the use of dependent sum is unavoidable in general.

5.4.3 Examples

We return to the examples based on the `Assoc` and `Union` types defined in Section
4.7. Suppose that, as in the previous examples, we intend to specialise the lookup
function knowing the variable names but not their values. What do the residual
programs look like? The following is a typical example. Suppose the static part of
the association list is

```
[("X",⊥), ("Y",⊥), ("Z",⊥)]
```

(using a list notation for an element of `Assoc`) and that we apply `lookup` to it with
index `"Y"`. The residual function would be,

```
lookup_1 (a,b,c) = b
```

The residual function now has three arguments whereas the original only had one.
This is an example of *arity raising* as described by Sestoft [Ses86] and Romanenko
[Rom88]. Sestoft reports that residual functions can have a significantly greater efficiency if arity raising is performed, but relied on hand placed annotations in the
program to obtain it. In contrast, Romanenko performed a post processing analysis
and achieved arity raising automatically. More recently, Mogensen [Mog89] used the
results of binding-time analysis for the same purpose. However, each of these approaches were fairly *ad hoc*. With dependent sum factorisation, arity raising arises as
a natural consequence of the theory.

Arity raising is not the only optimisation that dependent sum factorisation provides
automatically. Another is tag removal. Consider the numeric type,

```
type Num = Intg Int + Re Real + Comp (Real,Real)
```

(where `Real` is some suitably defined type of floating point numbers), and the following coercion function,

```
make_complex:Num->(Real,Real);
make_complex x = case x in
                    Intg n  -> (make_real (Intg n), 0.0)
                 || Re r    -> (r, 0.0)
                 || Comp c  -> c
                 end;
```

Suppose that binding-time analysis determines that the projection *TAG* specifies the static portion of the input to the function `make_complex`. Then the possible specialisations of `make_complex` are the functions,

```
make_complex_1:Int->(Real,Real);
make_complex_1 n = (make_real_4 n, 0.0);


make_complex_2:Real->(Real,Real);
make_complex_2 r = (r, 0.0);


make_complex_3:(Real,Real)->(Real,Real);
make_complex_3 c = c;
```

Not only has the run-time test been eliminated (and, presumably, another test in `make_real`) but so has the unnecessary packaging and unpackaging that occurred with complements. The arguments to the residual functions are optimal in that they contain no static information at all.

5.4.4 Dependent Sum Factorisation is a Division

We will close this chapter by showing that the dependent sum factorisation constitutes a division. As the domain is decomposed into a dependent sum, the dynamic function becomes an indexed family of functions—one for each static value. Define $\delta\ x = \delta_{\sigma x}\ x$ for a family of functions $\{\delta_a \mid a \in \sigma(\!(D)\!)\}$ where

$$\delta_a : \sigma^{-1}\{a\} \to B_a$$

is a bijection for each $a \in \sigma(\!(D)\!)$. The pairing function π must take a pair of values—in this case an element of a dependent sum—and reconstitute the original value. We define,

$$\pi\ (a,b) = \delta_a^{-1}\ b$$

These functions form a division. Before we can show this we need a lemma examining the interaction between the static and dynamic functions.

Lemma 5.6

If $a \in \sigma(D)$, and $b \in \delta_a(\sigma^{-1}\{a\})$, then $\sigma\ (\delta_a^{-1}\ b) = a$

Proof

As $b \in \delta_a(\sigma^{-1}\{a\})$ there exists a value $x \in \sigma^{-1}\{a\}$ such that $\delta_a^{-1}\ b = x$. But then $\sigma\ (\delta_a^{-1}\ b) = \sigma\ x = a$ as required. $\square$

Using this result we can prove,

Theorem 5.7

A triple (σ, δ, π) defined above forms a division.

Proof

We have to check the three conditions contained in the definition of a division. The first can be done directly.

$$
\begin{aligned}
\pi\ (\sigma\ x,\ \delta\ x) &= \delta_{\sigma x}^{-1}(\delta\ x) \\
&= \delta_{\sigma x}^{-1}(\delta_{\sigma x}\ x) \quad \text{[definition of } \delta] \\
&= x
\end{aligned}
$$

The other two conditions use the lemma.

$$
\begin{aligned}
\sigma\ (\pi\ (a, b)) &= \sigma\ (\delta_a^{-1}\ b) \\
&= a \quad\quad\quad\quad \text{[by the lemma]}
\end{aligned}
$$

$$
\begin{aligned}
\delta\ (\pi\ (a, b)) &= \delta\ (\delta_a^{-1}\ b) \\
&= \delta_{\sigma(\delta_a^{-1}\ b)}\ (\delta_a^{-1}\ b) \quad \text{[definition of } \delta] \\
&= \delta_a\ (\delta_a^{-1}\ b) \quad\quad\ \text{[by the lemma]} \\
&= b
\end{aligned}
$$

Thus (σ, δ, π) form a division as required. $\square$

This completes the theoretical development in the monomorphic case. We now know how to describe both static and dynamic data using projections, and have seen that it fits into Jones' general framework. In Chapter 7 we will consider the implications of moving to a polymorphic language, but before we do so we should check that the theory we have already seen may be realised in practice.

Chapter 6

Implementation

We have studied some of the theoretical aspects of using projections in binding-time analysis and how, again in theory, the dependent sum construction can be used to define the run-time arguments. In this chapter we will draw these threads together in the implementation of a projection-based partial evaluator. The current version is written in LML [Aug84] and not in PEL itself, so it is not yet self-applicable. Indeed there are still some problems about self-application of LML-like languages, which we discuss in the concluding chapter.

One slightly surprising feature is that the moderately complicated dependent sum construction turns out to be almost trivial to implement. In contrast, however, the binding-time analysis is fairly intricate because of the complexity involved in representing projections. Of necessity, parts of the following will interest only those intending to produce an implementation themselves. Anyone uninterested in the gory details should skim much of this chapter and turn to the final section where we develop the extended example.

6.1 General

A PEL program, as defined in Chapter 4, consists of type definitions followed by a series of function definitions. At the end of these is an expression to be evaluated. The value of this expression gives the value of the whole program. When we intend to partially evaluate a program we present it in exactly the same form except that the final expression is permitted to have free variables. These free variables indicate non-static data.

After partial evaluation, the residual program is in a similar form. It contains whichever type definitions are required, the residual functions with their associated type definitions and, finally, a residual expression. This expression contains the same free variables as before, but refers to the newly produced residual functions. Substituting any values for the free variables in both the original and residual programs will, on evaluation, produce the same answer.

Expressions are represented as trees constructed in the following data type.

```
type term =   Var String
            + Prod [term]
            + Constr String term
            + Call String term
            + RCall String term
            + Case term [(String, (term, term))]
```

Most of the tags are self explanatory. In the Case variant, the first term argument is the expression over which the case is performed. The names appearing in the association list are the various constructors appearing as patterns in the case statement. Paired with each name is a pair of expressions, the first of which is a possibly nested product of variables. This allows products to be decomposed. The second expression in the pair is the expression on the right hand side of the case statement. It is evaluated in the original environment augmented with the bindings implied by the pattern.

The function definitions are represented by an association list in which the function names are paired with a pair of expressions. As in the case statement, the first is a nested product of variables (which again allows products to be decomposed) and the second is the body of the function. This association list is present as a global value throughout the partial evaluator.

Currently only binding-time analysis is implemented; call annotations are inserted by hand. In the concrete syntax, a residual call is indicated by a # symbol preceding the function name. This gives rise to the distinction between the Call and the RCall tags above.

6.2   Binding-Time Analysis

The abstract objects manipulated in the binding-time analysis are projections and
hence functions. As the analysis contains tests for equality we may not manipulate
projections directly, but are forced to handle representations and implement functional equality by representational equality.

6.2.1   Representing Projections

By construction, each projection is finitely representable. However, for representational equality to be a correct implementation of functional equality, each projection
must have a canonical representation. This must be preserved by the various projection manipulating operations such as greatest lower bound.

Sums and Products

Projection sum and product are easy to model. Because we use a tagged sum with
named tags we represent a projection sum by an association list. The names in the
association list are the constructor names, and they are paired with the appropriate
projection to be applied to the summand. Over a sum, however, we may also have
the projection *ABS*. This gives us two possible variants in the representation type:
either Abs on its own, or Sum with its association list.

Products are even easier. A projection over a product is represented by a list of
projections, one for each of the factors. A product node in the tree is indicated by a
Prod constructor.

To give a uniform distinction between projection constructors and constructors in
other types, such as the type of expressions, we prefix the projection constructors
with the letter P. So far, this gives the tags PAbs, PSum and PProd.

Recursion

Some of the representation problems occur when representing projections over recursive domains. We indicate a recursive projection using a constructor PMu and use a

placeholder PRec in the parts of the tree where recursion takes place. This echoes the form $\mu\gamma.P(\gamma)$. To access the internal structure of the projection we must unfold the representation. This involves removing the PMu tag, and replacing every occurrence of PRec in the subtree with the original projection. This is performed by the function *unfold*.

Mathematically, it makes no difference to a projection whether it is unfolded or not. By the definition of the fixed point operator μ, the equation $P(\mu\gamma.P(\gamma)) = \mu\gamma.P(\gamma)$ always holds. Representationally, however, there is a difference between these two. We must ensure that, when we want to compare two recursive projections for equality, they are both folded.

The *fold* function from Chapter 4 is essentially the reverse of *unfold*, although this might not be obvious from the definition. When folding an arbitrary projection, the various parts that are to be replaced by the PRec placeholder may not all be the same. In this case we have to approximate and take the greatest lower bound. This is a direct result of the decision to use finite domains and, moreover, this is where finiteness is achieved. Replacing the parts with their greatest lower bound and then folding, produces the largest projection in the finite domain which is smaller than the original. Thus we see that the simpler but less constructive definition in Chapter 4 is the same as we have here. We may note that the two functions involved, namely *fold* and *unfold*, constitute the embedding/projection pair because *fold* ∘ *unfold* = *ID* and *unfold* ∘ *fold* ⊑ *ID*. They are maps between the finite domain of projections we use in the analysis and the domain of all projections.

Domain definitions in PEL may be mutually recursive. In order to represent these, it is not sufficient to have a single recursion marker. This is not because it is impossible to represent the projections doing so, but because it becomes extremely hard to keep uniqueness of representation. We arrange the domain definitions into mutually recursive blocks using a standard algorithm for finding the strongly connected components of a graph. A projection over one domain may involve projections over any of the other domains in the same component. If, in turn, any of those projections involve a projection in the original domain it will be the one we started with.

We enhance the PRec marker to include the name of a domain and likewise with the PMu constructor. The body of the projection is an association list in which domain names are paired with projections. All the domains in a single mutually recursive component appear in the list. To unfold a projection we extract the projection associated with the domain appearing as the first argument to PMu. All occurrences of

the PRec placeholder are replaced by the original projection with the first parameter
to PMu changed to the domain indicated by PRec.

For an example, consider the following mutually recursive domains,

```
type Listi = Nili + Consi (Int,Listb)
type Listb = Nilb + Consb (Bool,Listi)
```

These define lists whose elements alternate between integers and booleans. The projection over Listi that discards all the elements while retaining the structure is given
by

```
PMu "Listi"
  [("Listi",PSum [("Nili",PAbs),
                  ("Consi",PProd [PAbs, PRec "Listb"])]),
   ("Listb",PSum [("Nilb",PAbs),
                  ("Consb",PProd [PAbs, PRec "Listi"])])]
```

The corresponding projection over Listb is exactly the same except that the string
"Listb" appears as the first parameter to PMu. If we unfold the projection in the
example and access the projection associated with the second argument to Consi we
will obtain this projection—it will have exactly the same representation. Representational uniqueness is therefore preserved and function equality may be implemented
by representational equality.

The Representation Type

The datatype we use to represent projections may be defined as follows.

```
type Proj =   PProd [Proj]
            + PAbs
            + PSum [(String,Proj)]
            + PMu String [(String,Proj)]
            + PRec String
```

Because of the restrictions imposed by PEL on the form of type definitions we can
use a less general domain. In PEL, possible domain recursion is always followed by
a sum and this is the only place a sum may occur. The projections over a sum are
represented using `PAbs` or `PSum` so we may remove them from the generic `Proj` type
and place them in a type of their own. This allows the type checker to provide more
security guaranteeing for example, that we never compare a folded projection with
an unfolded one.

6.2.2   Computing Fixed Points

As shown by the equations in Chapter 4, the meanings of the abstract functions are
given by a greatest fixed point. Theoretically, this is computed across all functions
at all values simultaneously. However, even in fairly small example programs, a
direct implementation of this can be prohibitively expensive. It is not uncommon,
for example, for a domain of projections to contain 10 or more elements. A function
that maps between two such domains is a member of a domain containing some 10^{10}
elements (less actually because only the monotonic functions will be included). It is
clearly out of the question to attempt to find the fixed point by brute force.

Fortunately we do not need to know the value of the function for all of its possible
arguments. On the contrary it is usually sufficient to calculate it for only a few of
them. We calculate the value of the function at those points using the ideas of minimal
function graphs [JM86]. For each function we record argument/result pairs for only
those arguments we need. The arguments may arise directly from the analysis, or
they might be needed to calculate the value of another function. The starting values
come from the description of the expression at the end of the program. Where that
expression has free variables the `PAbs` projection tag is used.

Having obtained a table of (over-)approximations to some argument/result pairs of
some of the functions, the functions are repeatedly applied to the arguments using
the values in the table for any other function calls. These values are given by the
formula

$$f_{tab} \ x = \bigsqcap \{y \mid \exists z \ . \ x \sqsubseteq z, \ \{f : z \mapsto y\} \in tab\}$$

Whenever a function is used, it and its argument are added to the table paired with
the value computed for its result.

When finally an application of the functions leaves the table unchanged the argument/result pairs are correct and may be used in the analysis. Termination of the cycle is bound to occur because the abstract semantics is monotonic, and the domains are finite.

6.3 Specialisation

Much of the implementation of the specialisation function is unchanged from Chapter 2. The major difference concerns the presentation of static values and dynamic parameters. In Chapter 2 we assumed that, in the program, each function definition had two sets of parameters—one static the other dynamic—and that each function call had its arguments arranged likewise. This meant that it was very easy to construct the partial environment and to obtain parameters for the residual function.

In the current situation, with each function having a single argument that may contain both static and dynamic parts, we cannot hope to have the split performed beforehand. As we noted in Chapter 5, the generation of the residual domain is not a metastatic operation. Instead we use two functions to simulate the action of the functions σ and δ defined in Chapter 5.

We need some object to represent the use of $\bot$. We cannot use $\bot$ itself because it would lead to non-termination of the partial evaluator. We introduce a new summand into the `term` type, called `Bot`. The function `sigma` takes a function name and a partially static argument intended for that function. It uses the projection associated with the function retrieved from the (global) division to guide the replacement of the dynamic parts of the expression with `Bot`. This takes place within the `search` function mentioned in Chapter 2. The resulting pair, consisting of the function name and the static part of the argument, is returned in the result of `search` to be added to the `pending` list in the recursive call of `spec`. The specialisation function `spec` may be defined as follows.

```
spec [] done = []
spec ((f,s):pending) done
  = if    member done (f,s)
    then  spec pending done
    else
```

```
         ((f,s),(new_vs,new_body)) :
              spec (pending++new_fns) ((f,s):done)
     where
        (vs,body)   = lookup program f
        (s',vars')  = replace s vars
        new_vs      = delta s s'
        new_body    = eval (make_env vs s') body
        new_fns     = search new_body
```

The `replace` function uses a global list of variables (`vars`) and replaces each occurrence of `Bot` in the static argument with a fresh parameter. The resulting argument `s'` contains no occurrences of `Bot`, therefore.

To obtain the new variables for the residual program—this corresponds to calculating the inverse image of σ_f—we use the function `delta`. It is initially surprising that `delta` requires the original blanked out argument as well as the renamed one. However, recalling the mathematical construction of the δ function in Chapter 5, it will be immediately recognised as necessary. Unlike the δ function of Chapter 5, however, `delta` does not need to know which program function its argument belongs to. This is because we are using a generic value (expression) domain. All `delta` has to do is to produce a product containing all the parts of `s'` that are twinned with `Bot` in `s`. In this case, this will produce a product of variables.

Correspondingly, we must use `delta` at the original call of the function. Not only will the old function name be replaced with the name of the new residual function, but a new argument constructed from the dynamic parts of the original argument must be produced. This is the role of `delta`. Given the static information it will build a new argument which will match precisely the formal parameters of the residual function.

6.4   Example

In this chapter we have only touched on some of the more significant implementation issues. However, the action of the partial evaluator on other programs is more interesting than the text of the partial evaluator itself. Consequently, we will return to the example introduced in Chapter 2, and consider how it is affected by the use of a projection based partial evaluator.

In returning to the example we will see some gains but also some losses. It will come as no surprise that the state in the interpreter may be treated as a single parameter. No longer need it be implemented as two separate lists: a single association list suffices. The update function takes a name, a value, and an association list and returns a suitably altered association list. Working inside the structure, the binding-time analysis is able to recognise that the names are static while the values are dynamic.

Previously the value list appeared as a parameter to residual versions of run to be manipulated by residual versions of the update and lookup functions. Now, however, the values appear in the residual program not as a list but as part of a product. The residual versions of the lookup function are merely selections from the product and the residual versions of update map between products. There will be no harm in allowing these functions to be unfolded.

However, as indicated above, not everything has improved. In Chapter 2, the binding-time analysis completely ignored type information (indeed, the language could have been untyped). Each value was treated atomically so there was no difference between monotypes and instances of polytypes. At this stage in the thesis we can only handle monotypes, so all occurrences of polymorphism must be removed. As a consequence, we must introduce three different types of list, for example, one for commands, one for name/value pairs and one for integers. Each of these require their own monomorphic accessing functions. We will use the same names as before but with the type name appended.

Specialising the new interpreter to the example program from Chapter 2 (which finds the maximum value in the input) gives the residual program,

```
exec inp
  = run (0, hd_int inp, tl_int inp)

run (y,x,inp)
  = if    x > 0
    then  if    x > y
          then  run (x, hd_int inp, tl_int inp)
          else  run (y, hd_int inp, tl_int inp)
    else  Cons_int (y, Nil_int)
```

The result is now extremely close to a hand written version. There is little (if anything) that may be done in terms of improvement. A major gain has come from the automatic arity raising arising as a consequence of the dependent sum.

This gain is even more evident in the following example, involving a nested While.

```
Alloc X
  [ Read X,
    While (greater (var X) zero)
      [ Alloc Y
          [ Assign Y one,
            While (greater (var X) zero)
              [ Assign Y (multiply (var Y) (var x)),
                Assign X (subtract (var X) one) ],
            Write (var Y) ],
        Read X ],
    Write zero ]
```

The program maps a list of integers into a list of corresponding factorials. Both input and output lists are terminated by 0. A notable feature in this example is that we have chosen to allocate a variable within the outer While loop. This variable exists for one pass of the loop and is then deallocated. On the next pass it is reallocated and so on.

What does the result look like after partial evaluation? There are now two While loops and so there are two residual versions of run.

```
exec inp = run_1 (hd_int inp, tl_int inp)

run_1 (x,inp)
  = if    x>0
    then  run_2 (1, x, inp)
    else  Cons_int (0, Nil_int)

run_2 (y,x,inp)
  = if    x>0
    then  run_2 (y*x, x-1, inp)
    else  Cons_int (y, run_1 (hd_int inp, tl_int inp))
```

The residual program reflects very clearly the tail recursive structure of the interpreter. The two residual versions of `run` are in mutual tail recursion with each other. Once again, there is nothing in the residual program that is not essential to the computation.

The inner allocation of the `y` variable is reflected in the fact that `run_2` has three parameters whereas `run_1` has only two. What would be less efficient interpretively (because the `Alloc` would have to be interpreted each time around the loop) turns out to provide greater efficiency when compiled, for the outer function (`run_1`) would have three parameters even though one would not be *live*.

Let us not forget the fly in the ointment. Polymorphism is very important as a means for obtaining modularity. At the moment, every input program to the partial evaluator must be monomorphic, and every residual program will be monomorphic. In the example above this forced us to declare three different sorts of list. In the next chapter we explore how to extend our techniques to cope with polymorphism.

Chapter 7

Polymorphism

There are two almost separate issues to be addressed when we consider polymorphic languages: How to perform polymorphic binding-time analysis, and how to specialise polymorphic functions. We address both here.

Strachey identified two flavours of polymorphism [Str67] which he styled parametric and *ad hoc*. We will only consider parametric polymorphism, as arises in the widely used Hindley-Milner type system, for example. As *ad hoc* polymorphism may be reduced to parametric polymorphism by introducing higher-order functions [WB89], this decision is consistent with the thrust of the thesis where we have been considering a first-order language only.

A polymorphic function is a collection of monomorphic instances which, in some sense, behave the same way. Ideally, we would like to take advantage of this uniformity to analyse (and perhaps even specialise) a polymorphic function once, and then to use the result in each instance. Up to now the only work in polymorphic partial evaluation has been by Mogensen [Mog89]. However, with his polymorphic instance analysis each instance of a polymorphic function is analysed independently of the other instances and, as a result, a single function may be analysed many times.

To capture the notion of uniformity across instances Abramsky defined the notion of *polymorphic invariance* [Abr86]. A property is polymorphically invariant if, when it holds in one instance, it holds in all. Abramsky showed, for example, that a particular strictness analysis was polymorphically invariant. Unfortunately this does not go far enough. Polymorphic invariance guarantees that the result of the analysis of any monomorphic instance of a polymorphic function can be used in all instances, but not that the abstraction of the function can. An example of this distinction appears in [Hug89a].

A more promising avenue of research is suggested by category theory. In a first-order language, polymorphic functions turn out to be natural transformations in the category of (Scott) domains and continuous functions. In higher-order languages things are not so simple. Higher-order functions may be seen as dinatural transformations [BFSS87, FGSS88] but, unfortunately, these do not compose in the way natural transformations do, which limits their usefulness. Alternatively, generalising to transformations between structors (a generalisation of functors) seems more promising. These results turn out to be consequences of Reynold's original representation theorem for the polymorphic λ-calculus [Rey74]. This is developed by Wadler showing its application to "everyday theorems" [Wad89] and Abramsky has used these notions to greatly simplify the proof that strictness is polymorphically invariant [Abr88]—the contrast in readability between this and the original proof is dramatic.

In this thesis we have restricted ourselves to the first-order case, so we can treat polymorphic functions as natural transformations. Using this view we develop a theory of polymorphic binding-time analysis. The development is based heavily on Hughes' work in polymorphic strictness analysis [Hug89b]—an example of the cross fertilisation between the two analyses suggested in Chapter 3. We then discuss how to use the results to control the specialisation of polymorphic functions.

7.1 Semantic Properties of Polymorphism

Because typechecking takes place on the syntactic description of a function, polymorphism is usually understood to be a syntactic condition. Furthermore, it is quite possible for two functions having the same behaviour to have different degrees of polymorphism. The following two definitions of the identity function provide an example of this.

```
id  x = x

id' x = if true then x else 7
```

The first has type $id :: \forall t \, . \, t \rightarrow t$ whereas the second has type $id' :: Int \rightarrow Int$. So, while these two definitions denote the same function, they have distinct types. We deduce, therefore, that we cannot infer the type of a function from its semantic properties. We can, however, do the converse—some semantic properties of a function may be inferred from its type.

What sort of properties might we expect to be able to infer? Parametric polymorphism corresponds to a reuse of essentially the same function applied to objects of different types. The basic intuition behind such functions is that they do nothing to the polymorphic parts of their arguments except possibly discard or duplicate them. The very same *reverse* function, for example, will work identically on both lists of integers and lists of booleans. One way to express this is to imagine some function from integers to booleans being applied to each of the elements of a list. Because the behaviour of *reverse* is consistent across these types we could apply the function either before or after reversing the list without affecting the final result.

We can state this more generally. If a function is truly polymorphic (in the parametric sense) then we cannot trick it into altering its action by applying some coding function to the polymorphic parts of its argument prior to application. We would obtain the same result by applying the same coding function after application. The fact that the values of the polymorphic parts of the argument are different in each case will not result in a different behaviour. Of course this is still rather vague. For example we have not specified what we mean by the "polymorphic parts of an argument". We use the language of category theory to supply the necessary precision.

7.1.1   Types as Functors

We focus on one particular category, that of Scott domains with continuous functions which we denote by *Dom*. In a monomorphic language it is sufficient to model types by domains and program functions by continuous functions, but not if the language is polymorphic. It is useful to consider type constructors to see the necessary generalisation.

Type constructors, such as *List* or *Pair*, take one or more types and return a new type. They may be successfully modelled by functors. For example, from the domain of integers the *List* functor will return the domain of lists of integers. Functors act on arrows also. By defining the actions of the basic type constructions in the obvious way we can derive the action of any type constructor. So, for example, the action of *List* on arrows is given by *map* (the arrow (function) is applied to each element of the list). *List* is a functor $List : Dom \rightarrow Dom$ but as an arbitrary type constructor may have many arguments each will correspond to a functor $F : Dom^n \rightarrow Dom$ for some n.

Monomorphic types may be included in the same scheme. Such types, for example *Bool*, are functors $Bool : \mathbf{1} \rightarrow Dom$ where $\mathbf{1}$ is the category Dom^0 containing only the one point domain and the identity function. Any such functor has no opportunity to vary and so is constant. The image of the *Bool* functor, for example, is just the boolean domain. Types themselves, therefore, are no longer modelled by domains directly, but by functors.

Another monotype is *List Bool*. Because we treat monotypes such as *Bool* as functors $Bool : \mathbf{1} \rightarrow Dom$, the usual application of type constructors to types must be replaced by functor composition. Then *List Bool* (actually, $List \circ Bool$ of course) is also a functor $List\ Bool : \mathbf{1} \rightarrow Dom$.

7.1.2   Natural Transformations

Program defined functions are mappings between types. As types are modelled by functors, these functions should be modelled by transformations between functors. In fact, by natural transformations.

From their definition, we recall that a natural transformation $f : F \rightarrow G$ between functors is a collection of functions (which correspond to the monomorphic instances). If the source and target of F and G are the categories $\mathcal{D}$ and $\mathcal{E}$ respectively then for each object $D \in \mathcal{D}$ there is a corresponding function $f_D : FD \rightarrow GD$ in $\mathcal{E}$. These functions are uniform (or natural) in the following sense: If $\gamma : D \rightarrow D'$ is any function in $\mathcal{D}$ then the property that $G\gamma \circ f_D = f_{D'} \circ F\gamma$ must hold.

This captures precisely the notion that all the instances of a polymorphic function behave, in some sense, in the same way. It also expresses our intuition about applying coding (or other) functions to the polymorphic parts either before or after application of the polymorphic function without changing the result. In the case of *reverse*, for example, this means that $List\ f \circ reverse = reverse \circ List\ f$ for any function $f : X \rightarrow Y$, or to use more usual notation, that $map\ f \circ reverse = reverse \circ map\ f$.

To strengthen the intuition further we will consider a couple of examples. We have seen the implications for the *List* functor with the function *reverse*. Now consider the selection function *fst*. Its type is $fst : \forall s.\forall t.(s,t) \to s$. Expressed in the functor notation we could write $fst : Pair \to Fst$ where $Pair\ s\ t = (s,t)$ and $Fst\ s\ t = s$. Each of these are functors $Dom^2 \to Dom$. The naturality condition says that, for any continuous functions $\gamma : A \to B$ and $\delta : C \to D$, it must be the case that $Fst\ \gamma\ \delta \circ fst = fst \circ Pair\ \gamma\ \delta$. In other words, that $\gamma\ (fst\ (x,y)) = fst\ (\gamma\ x, \delta\ y)$ for all x,y.

All this works for monomorphic functions as well. Recall that types such as *Bool* or *Int* correspond to functors $Bool : 1 \to Dom$ and $Int : 1 \to Dom$. Consider an arbitrary function $f : Int \to Bool$, say. There is no polymorphism here as the function is purely monomorphic, so how does the naturality condition apply? The only function in the trivial category **1** (i.e Dom^0) is the identity function, which is mapped by any functor $1 \to Dom$ onto the identity function of the object picked out by the functor. Thus the naturality property reduces to the condition that f satisfies the equation $ID_{Bool} \circ f = f \circ ID_{Int}$. But this is no restriction at all, and so f may be any function. We conclude, therefore, that it is only when a function is not monomorphic that the naturality condition has any effect.

Depending on the emphasis at any particular time, we will either give the type of polymorphic functions in the usual notation or in functor notation. From the examples it should be clear that the two are interchangeable. The functor notation may be obtained from the usual type notation merely by abstracting over the quantified variables.

7.1.3 Polymorphism in Languages with Recursion

In most languages with recursion, $\bot$ is an element of every type. This gives rise to a necessary modification of the above. Consider the following function definition,

```
f x = f x
```

The function f is the constant $\bot$ function and has type $f : \forall t.t \to t$ or, equivalently, $f : Id \to Id$. For the naturality property to hold, that is, for $Id\ \gamma \circ f = f \circ Id\ \gamma$ to be true, γ must be strict. As we will see later this is the only extra condition required.

Domains together with the strict continuous functions form a sub-category of *Dom* which we write Dom_s. We change our view of type constructors and regard them as functors $Dom_s^n \to Dom_s$. We can do this since all our basic type constructions preserve strict functions and, therefore, so does any functor constructed from them.

However, there is a minor technicality. Regarding program defined functions as natural transformations between functors $Dom_s^n \to Dom_s$ only caters for *strict* polymorphic functions. But, as every functor $Dom_s^n \to Dom_s$ may be viewed as a functor $Dom_s^n \to Dom$ by inclusion, this problem may be solved by treating program defined functions as natural transformations between functors $Dom_s^n \to Dom$.

7.1.4 Functors and Projections

Before addressing polymorphic binding-time analysis we ought to note a couple of facts about the interaction of functors and projections. The functors that correspond to PEL types are of the form $F : Dom_s^n \to Dom$, so we need to define the projections in Dom_s^n.

The objects of Dom_s^n are n-tuples of objects of Dom and arrows, likewise, are n-tuples of Dom arrows. The projections in Dom_s^n are, therefore, simply n-tuples of projections in Dom. Most of the time we will use a single letter (typically γ) to refer to the whole tuple.

If F is a functor corresponding to a type expressible in PEL and if γ is a projection, then $F\gamma$ is also a projection. Idempotence follows from the composition property of functors, and dominance by the identity from the fact that all the functors are monotonic. Furthermore, because projections are weaker than the identity function, all projections are strict. This makes them suitable for commuting with polymorphic functions in the manner described above.

7.1.5 Polymorphic PEL

We have to extend PEL to allow for polymorphism. The only thing in the language that will change is the type system. In addition to the syntactic classes in Chapter 4 we will introduce the classes of type constructors and type variables,

$$
\begin{array}{lll}
\mathtt{F} & \in & \textit{Func} & \text{[Type Constructors]} \\
\mathtt{t} & \in & \textit{TVar} & \text{[Type Variables]}
\end{array}
$$

The revised (abstract) syntax of the language now caters for polymorphic types.

```
p  →  {D} {C d} e::T
d  →  f x = e
e  →  x
   |  (e₁,...,eₙ)
   |  c e
   |  f e
   |  case e in c₁ x₁ -> e₁ || ... || cₙ xₙ -> eₙ end
D  →  F {t} = c T {+ c T}
C  →  f :: T -> T
T  →  F T
   |  (T₁,...,Tₙ)
   |  t
```

Algebraic types have been replaced by type constructors applied to type variables. As we noted earlier, from any type expression we may obtain the corresponding functor by abstracting out the type variables. In the following we use F, G, H and K as variables ranging over functors.

Type Rules

The typechecking rules are much the same as before. The only additions are two rules that state that polymorphic functions (including constructors) and expressions have any type which is an instance of their general type. We express this using composition of functors, $F \circ H$ say. Because F may be a functor $Dom_s^n \to Dom$ where $n \neq 1$, the functor H must be of the form $Dom_s^m \to Dom_s^n$. Such functors may be expressed as a categorical product of functors $H_i : Dom_s^m \to Dom$ ($1 \leq i \leq n$) written $< H_1, \ldots, H_n >$.

$$x :: F \vdash x(i) :: F(i)$$

$$\frac{x :: F \vdash e_1 :: G_1 \quad \cdots \quad x :: F \vdash e_n :: G_n}{x :: F \vdash (e_1, \ldots, e_n) :: < G_1, \ldots, G_n >}$$

$$\frac{f :: G \to H \quad x :: F \vdash e :: G}{x :: F \vdash f\ e :: H}$$

$$\frac{c_i::G_i \to G \qquad x::F \vdash e::G_i}{x::F \;\vdash\; c_i\; e::G}$$

$$\frac{x::F \vdash e::H \qquad \forall i\,.\,(x::F, y_i::H_i \vdash e_i::G)}{x::F \;\vdash\; \texttt{case}\; e\; \texttt{in}\; c_1\; y_1 \texttt{->} e_1\; ||\; \ldots\; ||\; c_n\; y_n \texttt{->} e_n\; ::G}$$

$$\frac{f::G \to H}{f::G \circ K \to H \circ K}$$

$$\frac{x::F \vdash e::G}{x::F \circ K \vdash e::G \circ K}$$

In these rules we have departed from the notation of Chapter 4 and used the functor notation. Notice that the notation applies to variables as well as functions. A value v of type $F : Dom_s^n \to Dom$ may be seen as a natural transformation $v : \mathbf{1}^n \to F$, where $\mathbf{1}^n : Dom_s^n \to Dom$ is the constant functor picking out the terminal object of Dom (the one point domain). Using this notation simplifies the proof to come.

As before, we assume that a constructor c_i comes from a type definition of the form $G = c_1\; G_1 + \cdots + c_n\; G_n$ (using functor notation)[1]. For any object A or arrow f in Dom_s^n we have,

$$\begin{aligned} G\;A &= c_1\;(G_1\;A) + \cdots + c_n\;(G_n\;A)\\ G\;f &= c_1\;(G_1\;f) + \cdots + c_n\;(G_n\;f) \end{aligned}$$

Similarly, the product of functors is given by,

$$\begin{aligned} <G_1,\ldots,G_n> A &= (G_1\;A,\ldots,G_n\;A)\\ <G_1,\ldots,G_n> f &= G_1\;f \times \cdots \times G_n\;f \end{aligned}$$

as usual.

Semantics

Because the dynamic semantics of Chapter 4 was defined using a universal domain of values we can use it without change. The only difference arises in the way in which we

---

[1] Note that $+$ is domain separated-sum, and is not a categorical coproduct.

relate this semantics to the category of domains. In Chapter 4 we exhibited retracts between individual domains and the universal value space. Using these we were able to relate the action of a function on the universal domain with a particular arrow in the category of domains. If we desired we could do something similar. We would use indexed retractions to relate the action of a polymorphic function on the value space with the actions of its monomorphic instances in the category of domains. The details, however, are unnecessary for the following development.

7.1.6   Naturality

Functions defined in PEL correspond to natural transformations between functors $Dom_s^n \rightarrow Dom$. This property could be deduced from proofs about the second-order lambda calculus, and in particular from Reynolds' abstraction theorem, by exhibiting an appropriate relationship between PEL and the polymorphic λ-calculus. However, a direct proof is just as straightforward.

Theorem 7.1 (Naturality)
Let f be a function and F and G be functors defined in PEL. If $f :: F \rightarrow G$ is a valid typing of f then for all strict functions $\gamma : A \rightarrow B$ (where A and B are arbitrary)

$$ f \circ F\,\gamma \;=\; G\,\gamma \circ f $$

The proof is by fixed point induction over the definition of f ($= \phi[\![\,f\,]\!]$), but first we need a lemma. The lemma states that if everything works in some function environment (that is, that for any f, the function $\phi[\![\,f\,]\!]$ is a natural transformation) then any expression (seen as a function of its free variables, using the same function environment) is also a natural transformation.

Lemma 7.2
If $\mathbf{x} :: F \vdash \mathbf{e} :: G$ is a valid typing of $\mathbf{e}$, and if ϕ is some function environment such that for every function $\mathbf{g}$ appearing in $\mathbf{e}$ the valid typing $\mathbf{g} :: H \rightarrow K$ implies $\forall \gamma.\ \phi[\![\,\mathbf{g}\,]\!] \circ H\,\gamma = K\,\gamma \circ \phi[\![\,\mathbf{g}\,]\!]$, then for all strict functions $\gamma : A \rightarrow B$,

$$ \mathcal{E}_\phi[\![\,\mathbf{e}\,]\!]_{\{x \,\mapsto\, F\,\gamma\,v\}} \;=\; G\,\gamma\,(\mathcal{E}_\phi[\![\,\mathbf{e}\,]\!]_{\{x \,\mapsto\, v\}}) $$

Proof

The proof is by induction on the structure of **e**. There are five main cases to consider. Each case will be presented in the same way. First the type rule for the appropriate case will be given, followed by a demonstration of the lemma in the form required by the type rule.

Case: x(i)

The type rule is,

$$\mathbf{x} :: F \ \vdash \ \mathbf{x(i)} :: F(i)$$

So in this case $G = F(i)$. The corresponding derivation is,

$$
\begin{aligned}
\mathcal{E}_\phi[\![\mathbf{x(i)}]\!]_{\{x \mapsto F \ \gamma \ v\}} &= F(i) \ \gamma \ v(i) \\
&= F(i) \ \gamma \ (\mathcal{E}_\phi[\![\mathbf{x(i)}]\!]_{\{x \mapsto v\}})
\end{aligned}
$$

Case: $(\mathbf{e_1}, \ldots, \mathbf{e_n})$

The type rule is,

$$\frac{\mathbf{x} :: F \vdash \mathbf{e_1} :: G_1 \quad \cdots \quad \mathbf{x} :: F \vdash \mathbf{e_n} :: G_n}{\mathbf{x} :: F \ \vdash \ (\mathbf{e_1}, \ldots, \mathbf{e_n}) :: G}$$

where $G = < G_1, \ldots, G_n >$. The corresponding derivation is,

$$
\begin{aligned}
&\mathcal{E}_\phi[\![(\mathbf{e_1}, \ldots, \mathbf{e_n})]\!]_{\{x \mapsto F \ \gamma \ v\}} \\
&= (\mathcal{E}_\phi[\![\mathbf{e_1}]\!]_{\{x \mapsto F \ \gamma \ v\}}, \ldots, \mathcal{E}_\phi[\![\mathbf{e_n}]\!]_{\{x \mapsto F \ \gamma \ v\}}) \\
&= (G_1 \ \gamma \ \mathcal{E}_\phi[\![\mathbf{e_1}]\!]_{\{x \mapsto v\}}, \ldots, G_n \ \gamma \ \mathcal{E}_\phi[\![\mathbf{e_n}]\!]_{\{x \mapsto v\}}) \quad \text{[ind. hyp.]} \\
&= G \ \gamma \ (\mathcal{E}_\phi[\![\mathbf{e_1}]\!]_{\{x \mapsto v\}}, \ldots, \mathcal{E}_\phi[\![\mathbf{e_n}]\!]_{\{x \mapsto v\}}) \\
&= G \ \gamma \ \mathcal{E}_\phi[\![(\mathbf{e_1}, \ldots, \mathbf{e_n})]\!]_{\{x \mapsto v\}}
\end{aligned}
$$

Case: (g e)

The type rule is,

$$\frac{\mathbf{g} :: G \to H \qquad \mathbf{x} :: F \vdash \mathbf{e} :: G}{\mathbf{x} :: F \ \vdash \ \mathbf{g} \ \mathbf{e} :: H}$$

The corresponding derivation is,

$$
\begin{aligned}
\mathcal{E}_\phi[\![\mathsf{g}\ \mathsf{e}]\!]_{\{x\,\mapsto\,F\,\gamma\,v\}} &= \phi[\![\mathsf{g}]\!]\,(\mathcal{E}_\phi[\![\mathsf{e}]\!]_{\{x\,\mapsto\,F\,\gamma\,v\}}) \\
&= \phi[\![\mathsf{g}]\!]\,(G\ \gamma\,(\mathcal{E}_\phi[\![\mathsf{e}]\!]_{\{x\,\mapsto\,v\}})) \qquad \text{[ind. hyp.]} \\
&= H\ \gamma\,(\phi[\![\mathsf{g}]\!]\,(\mathcal{E}_\phi[\![\mathsf{e}]\!]_{\{x\,\mapsto\,v\}})) \qquad \text{[assumption]} \\
&= H\ \gamma\,(\mathcal{E}_\phi[\![\mathsf{g}\ \mathsf{e}]\!]_{\{x\,\mapsto\,v\}})
\end{aligned}
$$

Case: (c e)
The type rule is,

$$
\frac{\mathsf{c}_i::G_i \to G \qquad \mathsf{x}::F \vdash \mathsf{e}::G_i}{\mathsf{x}::F\ \vdash\ \mathsf{c}_i\ \mathsf{e}::G}
$$

where $G = c_1\ G_1 + \cdots + c_n\ G_n$. The corresponding derivation is,

$$
\begin{aligned}
\mathcal{E}_\phi[\![\mathsf{c}_i\ \mathsf{e}]\!]_{\{x\,\mapsto\,F\,\gamma\,v\}} &= c_i\,(\mathcal{E}_\phi[\![\mathsf{e}]\!]_{\{x\,\mapsto\,F\,\gamma\,v\}}) \\
&= c_i\,(G_i\ \gamma\ \mathcal{E}_\phi[\![\mathsf{e}]\!]_{\{x\,\mapsto\,v\}}) \\
&= G\ \gamma\,(c_i\ \mathcal{E}_\phi[\![\mathsf{e}]\!]_{\{x\,\mapsto\,v\}}) \\
&= G\ \gamma\,(\mathcal{E}_\phi[\![\mathsf{c}_i\ \mathsf{e}]\!]_{\{x\,\mapsto\,v\}})
\end{aligned}
$$

Case: (case e in $\cdots$ c$_i$ x$_i$ -> e$_i$ $\cdots$)
The type rule is,

$$
\frac{\mathsf{x}::F \vdash \mathsf{o}::H \qquad \forall i\ \ (\mathsf{x}::F, \mathsf{x}_i::H_i \vdash \mathsf{e}_i::G)}{\mathsf{x}::F\ \vdash\ \mathtt{case\ e\ in}\ \cdots\ \mathsf{c}_i\ \mathsf{x}_i\text{->}\mathsf{e}_i\ \cdots\ ::G}
$$

where $H = c_1\ H_1 + \cdots + c_n\ H_n$. The corresponding derivation is,

$$
\mathcal{E}_\phi[\![\mathtt{case\ e\ in}\ \cdots\ \mathsf{c}_i\ \mathsf{x}_i\ \text{->}\ \mathsf{e}_i\ \cdots\ ]\!]_{\{x\,\mapsto\,F\,\gamma\,v\}}
$$

$$
\begin{aligned}
=\quad & case\ \mathcal{E}_\phi[\![\mathsf{e}]\!]_{\{x\,\mapsto\,F\,\gamma\,v\}}\ in \\
& \qquad \vdots \\
& c_i\ v_i\ \Rightarrow\ \mathcal{E}_\phi[\![\mathsf{e}_i]\!]_{\{x\,\mapsto\,F\,\gamma\,v,\ x_i\,\mapsto\,v_i\}} \\
& \qquad \vdots
\end{aligned}
$$

$$= \quad case\ H\ \gamma\ (\mathcal{E}_\phi[\![\,\mathbf{e}\,]\!]_{\{x\,\mapsto\,v\}})\ in \qquad\qquad\qquad \text{[ind. hyp.]}$$

$$\vdots$$
$$c_i\ v_i\ \Rightarrow\ \mathcal{E}_\phi[\![\,\mathbf{e}_i\,]\!]_{\{x\,\mapsto\,F\ \gamma\ v,\ x_i\,\mapsto\,v_i\}}$$
$$\vdots$$

$$= \quad case\ \mathcal{E}_\phi[\![\,\mathbf{e}\,]\!]_{\{x\,\mapsto\,v\}}\ in \qquad\qquad\qquad \text{[meaning of } case]$$

$$\vdots$$
$$c_i\ v_i\ \Rightarrow\ \mathcal{E}_\phi[\![\,\mathbf{e}_i\,]\!]_{\{x\,\mapsto\,F\ \gamma\ v,\ x_i\,\mapsto\,H_i\ \gamma\ v_i\}}$$
$$\vdots$$

$$= \quad case\ \mathcal{E}_\phi[\![\,\mathbf{e}\,]\!]_{\{x\,\mapsto\,v\}}\ in \qquad\qquad\qquad \text{[ind. hyp.]}$$

$$\vdots$$
$$c_i\ v_i\ \Rightarrow\ G\ \gamma\ (\mathcal{E}_\phi[\![\,\mathbf{e}_i\,]\!]_{\{x\,\mapsto\,v,\ x_i\,\mapsto\,v_i\}})$$
$$\vdots$$

$$= \quad G\ \gamma\ \left(\begin{array}{l} case\ \mathcal{E}_\phi[\![\,\mathbf{e}\,]\!]_{\{x\,\mapsto\,v\}}\ in \\ \qquad \vdots \\ c_i\ v_i\ \Rightarrow\ \mathcal{E}_\phi[\![\,\mathbf{e}_i\,]\!]_{\{x\,\mapsto\,v,\ x_i\,\mapsto\,v_i\}} \\ \qquad \vdots \end{array} \right) \qquad [G\ \gamma\ \text{strict}]$$

$$= \quad G\ \gamma\ (\mathcal{E}_\phi[\![\,\texttt{case e in}\ \cdots\ \texttt{c}_i\ \texttt{x}_i\ \texttt{->}\ \texttt{e}_i\ \cdots\ ]\!]_{\{x\,\mapsto\,v\}})$$

In order to complete the proof we must consider the instance rules also. If $f : F \to G$ is a natural transformation from $F : Dom_s^n \to Dom$ to $G : Dom_s^n \to Dom$ then it is also a natural transformation from $F \circ K : Dom_s^m \to Dom$ to $G \circ K : Dom_s^m \to Dom$ where K is some functor $K : Dom_s^m \to Dom_s^n$. A simple calculation suffices.

$$\begin{aligned} f \circ ((F \circ K)\gamma) &= f \circ (F\ (K\gamma)) \\ &= (G\ (K\gamma)) \circ f \qquad \text{[naturality]} \\ &= ((G \circ K)\gamma) \circ f \end{aligned}$$

as required. The same calculation holds for values, as they may be treated as natural transformations from $\mathbf{1}^n$ to appropriate functors. This completes the proof. $\quad\square$

The function environment ϕ used in the lemma need not necessarily be the complete function environment defined by the program, of course. When we use the lemma in the following proof, ϕ will be a finite approximation to the complete environment.

Proof (naturality)

We have to prove that if f is a function and F and G are functors defined in PEL such that $f :: F \to G$ is a valid typing of f, then for all strict functions $\gamma : A \to B$ (where A and B are arbitrary)

$$f \circ F\,\gamma \;=\; G\,\gamma \circ f$$

The proof is by fixed point induction over the definition of ϕ. From the static semantics, $\phi = \mathit{fix}\,(\lambda\phi\,.\,\{\mathbf{f}_1 \mapsto \lambda v.\mathcal{E}_\phi[\![\,\mathbf{e}_1\,]\!]_{\{x_1 \mapsto v\}}\,,\dots,\;\mathbf{f}_n \mapsto \lambda v.\mathcal{E}_\phi[\![\,\mathbf{e}_n\,]\!]_{\{x_n \mapsto v\}}\,\})$ where the function definitions in the program are of the form $\mathbf{f}_i\;\mathbf{x}_i = \mathbf{e}_i$. As in earlier proofs we write $\{\phi_i\}$ for the Kleene chain approximating ϕ (then, by the definition of fix, $\phi = \bigsqcup_{i=0}^{\infty}\{\phi_i\}$) and use f_n to denote $\phi_n[\![\,\mathbf{f}\,]\!]$. There are three cases for the fixed point induction.

Case: base

$$
\begin{aligned}
f_0 \circ F\,\gamma &= \lambda x.\bot \circ F\,\gamma \\
&= \lambda x.\bot \\
&= G\,\gamma \circ \lambda x.\bot \quad [G\,\gamma \text{ strict}] \\
&= G\,\gamma \circ f_0
\end{aligned}
$$

Case: inductive

Suppose that the definition of f is given by $\mathbf{f}\;\mathbf{x} = \mathbf{e}$. Then,

$$
\begin{aligned}
f_{n+1} \circ F\,\gamma &= \lambda v.\mathcal{E}_{\phi_n}[\![\,\mathbf{e}\,]\!]_{\{x \mapsto v\}} \circ F\,\gamma \\
&= \lambda v.\mathcal{E}_{\phi_n}[\![\,\mathbf{e}\,]\!]_{\{x\,\mapsto\, F\,\gamma\,v\}} \\
&= G\,\gamma \circ \lambda v.\mathcal{E}_{\phi_n}[\![\,\mathbf{e}\,]\!]_{\{x\,\mapsto\, v\}} \quad [\text{lemma and ind. hyp.}] \\
&= G\,\gamma \circ f_{n+1}
\end{aligned}
$$

Case: limit

$$
\begin{aligned}
f \circ F\,\gamma &= (\bigsqcup_{i=0}^{\infty}\{f_i\}) \circ F\,\gamma \\
&= \bigsqcup_{i=0}^{\infty}\{f_i \circ F\,\gamma\} \quad [\text{defn. of } \bigsqcup] \\
&= \bigsqcup_{i=0}^{\infty}\{G\,\gamma \circ f_i\} \\
&= G\,\gamma \circ \bigsqcup_{i=0}^{\infty}\{f_i\} \quad [\text{continuity}] \\
&= G\,\gamma \circ f
\end{aligned}
$$

which completes the proof. $\square$

It is instructive to note where the various restrictions played their part. The strictness of the commuting function γ was essential in the inductive base case. In a language without recursion the inductive proof would not be required and without it there would be no need for strictness. Indeed, if $\perp$ were inexpressible in PEL then program functions would be natural transformations over the usual category of domains with arbitrary continuous functions. When $\perp$ is expressible, *case* expressions commute only with strict functions, hence an appeal to strictness in the lemma also.

The restriction that PEL functions be first-order is used in the proof of the lemma in the function case. It is because the meaning of a function can be expressed in terms of ϕ without reference to the values of variables, that the inductive hypothesis may be used to effect the commutativity essential to the proof. If functions could be arbitrary expressions (as is the case in a higher-order language) then the need to reference variables to obtain their meaning would stop the proof from going through, and a more general theorem would be required.

7.2   Polymorphic Analysis Theorem

We will see later that we can use polymorphic projections (projections that satisfy the semantic polymorphism condition) to describe the results of binding-time analysis of polymorphic functions. Such projections interact cleanly with the program functions as the following theorem (taken directly from strictness analysis, [Hug89b]) shows.

Theorem 7.3 (Polymorphic Analysis)
If $f : F \to G$ is polymorphic, and if $\alpha : G \to G$ and $\beta : F \to F$ are polymorphic projections such that $\alpha \circ f = \alpha \circ f \circ \beta$, then for any projection $\gamma : X \to X$

$$(\alpha_X \circ G\ \gamma) \circ f_X = (\alpha_X \circ G\ \gamma) \circ f_X \circ (\beta_X \circ F\ \gamma)$$

Proof
We will use the equivalent statement of safety.

$$
\begin{aligned}
(\alpha_X \circ G\ \gamma) \circ f_X &= \alpha_X \circ f_X \circ F\ \gamma && \text{[naturality]} \\
&\sqsubseteq (f_X \circ \beta_X) \circ F\ \gamma && \text{[assumption]} \\
&= f_X \circ (\beta_X \circ F\ \gamma)
\end{aligned}
$$

as required. $\square$

7.2.1 Approximate Factorisation of Projections

The practical consequence of the theorem is to improve the efficiency of binding-time analysis. Each function f has an abstract version $f^{\#}$ associated with it, with the property that $f^{\#}\beta \circ f \sqsubseteq f \circ \beta$ for any projection β. By the above theorem it is clear that we can define $f^{\#}(\beta_X \circ F\gamma) = (f^{\#}\beta)_X \circ G\gamma$. If we restrict ourselves to projections which may be factorised in this way then $f^{\#}$ will be fast to compute. In general there are far fewer polymorphic projections than monomorphic. For example, over the *List* functor we use only three polymorphic projections (ABS, $List\ ABS^2$, and ID) but over some particular list domain we have these and more. Thus, instead of having to find a fixed point in some large domain we can do as well by computing it in a far smaller domain. There is a second advantage, namely that the results of the analysis are not restricted to one particular instance but may be used in all. Separately computing $f^{\#}$ for each monomorphic instance loses on two accounts—the size of the domains, and the repeated work.

To discover whether the method will be generally applicable, however, we must ask whether it is sufficient to consider only those projections that can be factorised in this way. This is certainly the case with the *List* functor. In designing finite domains of projections we chose to treat each recursive level alike. Thus all the projections over lists may be decomposed into a projection that works on all the elements identically (and only on the elements) and a projection which (possibly) alters the list structure.

The same is not necessarily true in all cases. For example, consider a function $f : \forall t.(t,t) \to t$. As the only polymorphic projections over f's source functor are ABS and ID (given by (ABS, ABS) and (ID, ID)), the only projections that may be factorised as above treat both elements of the pair in the same way. However, in any particular instance of f, for example $f_{Bool} : (Bool, Bool) \to Bool$, there is nothing that constrains the two elements to be equally defined or otherwise. Indeed we might commonly expect the first to be defined and the second not, or vice versa. What can we do in such cases? The answer is that instead of demanding an exact factorisation we find an approximate factorisation. Thus for any $\delta : FA \to FA$ we find projections $\beta : F \to F$ (polymorphic) and $\gamma : A \to A$ such that $\beta \circ F\gamma \sqsubseteq \delta$. Such an approximation is safe because we are underestimating the available information. In the example above, a projection $(\gamma, \delta) : (Bool, Bool) \to (Bool, Bool)$ would be replaced by $(\gamma \sqcap \delta, \gamma \sqcap \delta)$. While there is information loss here it often turns out to

---

[2]This has been called $STRUCT$ elsewhere.

be minimal. In some cases, exactly the same information loss arises anyway but by another route. The primitive operator *if* is a good example of this as we now show.

The type of *if* is $if : \forall t.(Bool, t, t) \rightarrow t$. Written using the functor notation, it is $if : Cond \rightarrow Id$ where $Cond\ t = (Bool, t, t)$. There are four polymorphic projections from *Cond* to itself. The *Bool* field may either be blanked (using ABS_{Bool}) or left intact, and likewise for the polymorphic parts (using polymorphic *ID* and *ABS*). The table for the polymorphic abstract function $if^{\#}$ is below.

α	$if^{\#}\alpha$
$ABS_{Bool} \times ABS \times ABS$	ABS
$ABS_{Bool} \times ID \times ID$	ABS
$ID_{Bool} \times ABS \times ABS$	ABS
$ID_{Bool} \times ID \times ID$	ID

An arbitrary projection, $(\eta \times \gamma \times \delta)$ say, over the argument to an instance of *if* is decomposed into the composition of either $(ABS_{Bool} \times ID \times ID)$ or $(ID_{Bool} \times ID \times ID)$ (depending on whether $\eta = ABS_{Bool}$ or not) with the projection $Cond\ (\gamma \sqcap \delta)$. Then, the result of applying $if^{\#}$ is either $ABS \circ (\gamma \sqcap \delta)$ or $ID \circ (\gamma \sqcap \delta)$ respectively, that is, either ABS or $\gamma \sqcap \delta$. Depending on whether the boolean is static or not, the result is either completely dynamic, or is static where both branches are static. But this is exactly the same result that separate analysis of each monomorphic instance would obtain!

Neither type checking nor binding-time analysis is based on program values. The fact that it was necessary to take an approximation to obtain the factorisation (which is type based) corresponds to the fact that binding-time analysis cannot determine which of the branches of an *if* may be returned and so must assume the worst. It might be hoped that there is a more general result here—possibly that the approximate factorisation will *never* do any worse than the binding-time analysis would anyway. After all, both have access to the same information. Unfortunately this is not the case. Consider the function,

```
f (x,y) = fst (x, if true x y)
```

The type of this function is $f : \forall t.(t, t) \rightarrow t$ or, in functor notation, $f : \Delta \rightarrow Id$ where $\Delta\ t = (t, t)$. If we analyse an instance of f polymorphically, using two projections $\gamma, \delta : A \rightarrow A$ say, we must approximate the projection (γ, δ) by $\Delta\ (\gamma \sqcap \delta)$. The result of applying the abstract function is, unsurprisingly, $\gamma \sqcap \delta$. If, on the other hand, we choose to analyse f monomorphically, then we do not need an approximation step, and will obtain γ as the result. So, this example shows that, even though both type checking and binding-time analysis have access to the same information, the binding-time analysis is able to make fuller use of it. Recently, a type checking approach to binding-time analysis has been developed [Gom89]. It would be interesting to see whether the more general result we hoped for above holds in this case.

The counter-example is so contrived that we might think the problem has no practical significance. However it is closely related to an important observation. If a function is given a type which is not as general as it could be, then unnecessary information loss may occur. For example, if the function *fst* is given the type $fst : \forall t.(t, t) \rightarrow t$ rather than its fully general type, then the result will always need to take both parameters into account. In the example above, the *if* expression is used solely as an artificial constraint upon the type of the function. Experience suggests that, where the type is not constrained artificially but only out of necessity (as in the *if* example), the information loss is minimal. A far greater source of information loss arises from the use of finite domains of projections, as these cause every recursive level to be treated identically.

7.3   Polymorphic Specialisation

Binding time analysis is not the only beneficiary from taking polymorphism into account. The process of function specialisation may also be improved by using such information.

If we have a polymorphic function which we wish to specialise to part of its argument we have two choices. Either all the available information can be used in the specialisation, or only the parts of the information over which the function is not polymorphic. So long as efficiency is not lost the latter is clearly better. The residual function will be more general than in the former case, and will retain a polymorphic type. Consequently, we will need to produce fewer residual functions, and each may be used in many situations. The residual functions will be at least as polymorphic as the source function because no instance information is supplied.

Is efficiency lost? To answer this we must consider what might happen to polymorphic values within the body of a polymorphic function. There are two possibilities. Either the values appear in the result of the function, possibly as part of a data structure, or, alternatively, they are provided in an argument to another function. In this case the typechecking rules guarantee that this other function must itself be polymorphic. In neither case, therefore, can any significant computation take place. The apparent circularity of this argument may be removed by noticing that the polymorphic primitives can themselves do no processing on the polymorphic parts of their arguments (e.g. `fst`). Again, this is an appeal to the basic intuition about polymorphic functions. We conclude, therefore, that because the source function is (by assumption) parametrically polymorphic, the only possible loss of efficiency is that some values will be passed as parameters rather than appearing as in-line constants. Any increase in cost is restricted merely to an increase in the number of parameters. This penalty is expected to be minimal on most implementations. It should be re-emphasised that this whole argument depends on the source language being first-order and having parametric polymorphism only.

Let us consider an example, that of the standard `lookup` function. It is sometimes ascribed the type $lookup : \forall n \forall v.([(n, v)], n) \to v$. However, this requires the use of a "polymorphic" equality function. The behaviour of such a function can easily be altered by coding its arguments in a non-one-to-one manner. Following the argument above, therefore, this brand of polymorphism is *ad hoc* and not parametric. If we replace the overloaded equality function with a monomorphic version, then the actual type of the *lookup* function is $lookup : \forall v.([(Name, v)], Name) \to v$ for some fixed type *Name*.

We consider a case where the values are static but the names are dynamic. When specialising an interpreter we might expect the reverse, of course, but in other contexts the situation we describe could arise. From the discussion above we recognise that even though the values are actually present we will gain nothing by using them in the specialisation. As the value part is polymorphic we treat it as if it were dynamic.

Suppose we specialise *lookup* to the value `([(x,3),(y,4)],z)` where `x`, `y` and `z` are dynamic variables. The values are indeed static—they are provided as constants. Using the approach outlined above we obtain the residual function

```
lookup_1 (a,b,c,d,e) = if eq_Name a e then
                       b
                   else if eq_Name c e then
                       d
                   else fail
```

and the original function call is replaced by the call, `lookup_1 (x,3,y,4,z)`. The
same residual function `lookup_1` is suitable for any two-list. Contrast this with the
situation that would have arisen if the values were used in the specialisation. Then
the residual function would have been

```
lookup_1 (a,b,c) = if eq_Name a e then
                   3
                   else if eq_Name c e then
                   4
                   else fail
```

Granted that there are two fewer parameters, but this residual version of `lookup` is
only suitable for this particular association list. Any other list, even if it had two
elements, would require a new residual function to be produced.

Consequences for Binding-Time Analysis

If a polymorphic function is only ever to receive the non-polymorphic parts of its
argument during specialisation, then its static projection will have *ABS* in the polymorphic positions. Because *ABS* is polymorphic, this means that the projection
associated with a polymorphic function is itself polymorphic. Therefore, we only
need to consider a finite domain of polymorphic projections when calculating the
projection associated with a polymorphic function. There are, of course, fewer of
these than projections over arbitrary instance types. This means the search space is
smaller giving an additional benefit for binding-time analysis.

7.4   Representing Polymorphic Projections

Very little change is required in order to implement the methods of this chapter. Of
course the parser must be altered, the typechecker must now handle polymorphism,
and so on, but such things are standard.

The datatype used to represent polymorphic projections is much the same as before.
The recursion former `PMu` has an extra parameter consisting of a list of projections
in order to simulate the form $\beta \circ F\gamma$. The list of projections corresponds to γ (which

may, in general, be an n-tuple of projections, i.e. a projection in Dom^n). Type variables in the type definitions lead to variables in the projection structure (PParm). On unfolding, the particular projections are substituted for the corresponding parameters.

The complete datatype is,

```
type Proj =   PProd [Proj]
          + PAbs
          + PSum [(String,Proj)]
          + PMu String [(String,Proj)] [Proj]
          + PRec String
          + PParm String
```

If a projection parameter is encountered within the specialiser, it is treated like PAbs. This implements the principle that polymorphic parts of an argument are to be discarded. Further details of the implementation may be found in the appendices.

7.5   Example

It should be fairly clear by now how the methods of the chapter affect the extended example. The ugliness from Chapter 6 (the many list types) has gone, as we are able to write the interpreter using polymorphic lists, and obtain polymorphic lists in the residual program. In addition, the advantages developed in this chapter will apply, so the analysis of functions such as *append* will be improved (it will happen once only, and the result will be obtained more quickly). However, the interpreter was originally a monomorphic program in that the only polymorphic structures appeared as monomorphic instances. As a result, the residual programs are little better than their monomorphic counterparts. We should not be surprised at this: the main purpose of the polymorphism material was to allow more freedom in the *source* program, to allow polymorphism (an important modularity technique) to be used. A complete listing of the example is given as the last section of Appendix C.

If the interpreter had many different types of list or perhaps various kinds of trees that appeared in residual programs, then the improvement in moving to the methods of this chapter would be more visible. Not only would the analysis benefit from taking polymorphism into account, but the residual programs would contain polymorphic functions manipulating the various structures. In the monomorphic case, we would have many separate instances of these functions.

Chapter 8

Conclusion

In conclusion we will summarise the previous chapters so that we can assess the work within a wider context and see what remains to be done.

8.1 Appraisal

After introducing partial evaluation and its potential as a programming tool in Chapter 1, we moved on in Chapter 2 to review the DIKU implementation strategy which was simple yet powerful. Values are treated atomically—a value is either static or dynamic—but even so, such partial evaluators have been used successfully in many experiments. We discussed the nature of binding-time analysis, and included an argument that it is crucial if self-application is to be attempted.

In an attempt to reach inside data structures, to express a greater degree of separation of binding-times, we used domain projections to indicate static data. There were various advantages associated with this. Firstly, there is a very natural sense in which a projection can capture the absence of information—dynamic data is mapped to $\perp$. Secondly, it turned out to be easy to generate finite domains of projections tailored to each data type. Thirdly, projection-based analysis has already received attention and, as a backward analysis at least, is fairly well understood. Indeed, we discovered an equivalence between binding-time analysis and the more familiar strictness analysis, in that both analyses use the same safety condition. Finally, as projections are semantic objects with a semantically expressed safety condition, they need no interpretation to fit with semantically derived methods, two of which we studied in detail later in the thesis.

In Chapter 4, we defined a projection-based binding-time analysis, and proved the safety of the equations. Because binding-time analysis begins initially with information about the input to the program, the analysis was a forwards analysis. This made an interesting contrast with projection-based strictness analysis which propagates demand, and so is a backwards analysis. The existence of two such equivalent analyses promises to lead to further insights into the relationship between forward and backward analyses.

The definition of static projections and the associated binding-time analysis described static values—those that are present during partial evaluation. In Chapter 5, therefore, we turned our attention to run-time values. Motivated by the need to express the origin of the run-time parameter, we explored two decomposition theorems, one providing approximate factorisation, the other exact. In the latter case, the use of dependent sum as a generalisation of product allowed us to express mathematically the familiar techniques of arity raising and tag removal. Consequently, these optimisations need no longer be seen as arbitrary or *ad hoc*, but as natural outgrowths of the theory. That the decomposition theorem is built around projections is no accident. Their role in the decomposition is motivated by the same intuition that gave rise to their use in binding-time analysis in the first place, and provides evidence of the value of using semantic objects to express binding times.

Chapter 6 brought the threads of the previous chapters together in a working projection-based partial evaluator. The extended example showed significant improvements over the situation in Chapter 2, but also some degradation: all types were monomorphic. This prohibited the use of polymorphic lists, for example, which we had been able to use in the simpler (untyped) setting of Chapter 2. We turned our attention, therefore, to polymorphism.

Semantic characterisations of polymorphism have become popular recently. They seem to open up powerful proof methods, in addition to providing new intuitions as to the nature of polymorphic functions. Again, the advantage of using a semantic characterisation of binding time analysis became clear as we were able to make immediate use of these new insights. In particular, we were able to apply Hughes' polymorphic analysis result directly, a result originally intended for strictness analysis. Thus polymorphic types fitted neatly into the framework we had previously constructed.

The most important consequence of this is the most obvious, namely that the partial evaluator is actually able to specialise polymorphic programs. This removes one of the restrictions previously placed on the form of the input program. Binding time analysis of polymorphic functions is cheaper than the analysis of monomorphic instances because the respective domains are smaller, and as the specialised versions of polymorphic functions are themselves polymorphic, the residual functions may be used in many instances.

8.2 Development

The story does not end here, of course. In particular, there are still many restrictions on the form of the input program. For example, it is not yet clear how to extend the methods described here to cater for higher-order functions. This is by no means the only shortcoming. In this section, we consider some other areas open to improvement.

8.2.1 Finiteness

In Chapter 2, we noted that a division produced by binding-time analysis should be both congruent and finite. It is possible to capture congruence quite well using an abstract interpretation, but finiteness does not seem to be so straightforward. In lazy or higher-order languages another problem arises that is very closely related, that of comparing partial or infinite objects. This arises in the following situation. Suppose there is a call of a function f with argument y. Further suppose that we have already produced specialised versions of f, specialised to values x_1, x_2, etc. We need to know whether the static part of y is equal to the static part of any of the x's. To be of any use, this test must be computable. That is, we must guarantee that the test $\sigma\ y = x_1$ cannot have the result $\perp$ (here $=$ is computable rather than mathematical equality). If any of the static values are infinite, then mathematical equality is not computable. In order to ensure that this does not arise, the values we compare must be finite and, furthermore, must be maximal in the domain of static values. If the value is not maximal then again we would need a non-monotonic (hence non-computable) equality test. Stating this another way, any $\perp$ appearing in the result of $\sigma\ y$ must have been introduced by σ.

It is possible to discover finiteness using abstract interpretation. In Chapter 3 we

noted that congruence is an over-estimate of the halting problem. Finiteness requires
an under estimate of the same problem. That is, the answer LOOPS should be returned
if there is any possibility of non-termination. Recognising this, Mycroft introduced
two analyses, # and ♭, the former being strictness analysis, the latter termination
analysis. Strictness analysis has become very popular, while termination analysis has
not. The reason for this is that, while abstract interpretation can give excellent results
for strictness analysis (and hence congruence analysis), it gives very poor results for
termination analysis. An example will help to show why. Consider the function

```
f (x,y) = if x=0 then y else f (x-1,y)
```

defined over the natural numbers. It is clearly strict in both x and y for if $\perp$ is substituted for either parameter the result is also $\perp$. Even the earliest strictness analysis
techniques could discover this. In contrast, consider the corresponding termination
question. If non-$\perp$ values are substituted for both x and y, is the result also non-$\perp$?
By inspection the result is obviously "yes". However more mental work is required to
discover this. In particular one has to consider the range of possible values for x to
check that, whatever its value is, the value 0 will be reached in the recursion. Thus,
the function will only return a non-$\perp$ value if the values for x and y are non-$\perp$ and
if *the recursion finishes*. Such a distinction does not need to be made for strictness
analysis. If the value for y is $\perp$ then the result could be $\perp$ either because the recursion terminates and $y = \perp$, or because the recursion does not terminate. We do not
need to distinguish between these cases and, in particular, never need to ensure that
recursion is finite.

At first it seems quite puzzling that strictness and termination are not equally easy to
discover when one is the dual of the other. The reason is that there is an asymmetry
in the language semantics: recursive definitions are given by least fixed point. If, in
some topsy turvy world, recursive definitions were given by greatest fixed point then
termination would be the easy property to discover and strictness would be hard. In
the example above, if neither x nor y were $\perp$ then either y would be returned (if the
recursion finished) or else the recursion would not finish and the result would be $\top$.
In neither case is the result $\perp$. However, in the real world we have no option but to
use least fixed point, so termination analysis will always be harder than strictness.
In partial evaluation terms, this means that finiteness will be harder to ensure than
congruence. This certainly accords with experience.

8.2.2 Values from Residual Functions

A residual function is produced whenever a residual call is encountered. The idea behind making a function residual is that the function call cannot be unfolded safely. As a consequence, it may be thought that no result may be obtained from a residual call, for how can a result be obtained without unfolding? However, there may be sufficient input to the function to cause some part of the result to be static even though the function as a whole cannot be unfolded. Unfolding could take place to allow the static part to be computed, while a residual function is produced to generate the remainder.

Unless the binding-time analysis handles partially static structures, we will only obtain trivial results. In Chapter 3, we argued that it is unreasonable to expect the input to a function to be pre-divided into static and dynamic parts. The argument is even more forceful regarding the result of a function. Thus, we must perform the factorisation ourselves using whichever method used in the partial evaluator. Before discussing the case of dependent sum factorisation, we will consider the complement factorisation. This will give us insight into what we should expect in the more complicated situation.

Suppose we have a function $f : X \rightarrow Y$ where we are able to factorise X into the product $A \times B$ in which A contains the static part of the input. Suppose also that Y factorises into the product $C \times D$ with C containing the static part of the result. The C part of the result must be determined, therefore, by the A part of the argument alone. Now, we know that

$$X \rightarrow Y \;\cong\; A \times B \rightarrow C \times D \;\cong\; (A \times B \rightarrow C) \times (A \times B \rightarrow D)$$

but because the C value is determined by the A value, we do not need to consider the whole space $(A \times B \rightarrow C) \times (A \times B \rightarrow D)$ but only the part isomorphic to $(A \rightarrow C) \times (A \times B \rightarrow D)$. The first component of such a pair of functions gives the static result and may be unfolded, whereas the second gives the dynamic result. It will not be unfolded but the function will be specialised to the A value leaving a residual function in its place.

Manipulating products in this way is not new. In his thesis Mogensen gives the syntactic translations needed to carry it out [Mog89] and produces independent textual definitions of each function. This is performed as a preprocessing phase to *mix* and results in a program in which the data can be treated atomically. This allows the original *mix* to be used. Because it is a preprocessing phase, only metastatic information is used to drive the transformation. As a result, the type of the residual function is also determined metastatically, in this case it will be $B \to D$, which means, for example, that lists will remain as lists rather than tuples and that all tags must remain.

We can perform similar factorisations using dependent sum. Again we assume a function $f : X \to Y$ with the static part of the input being given by A, in this case as defined by a projection α. The static part of the result is given by C and defined by a projection β where $\beta \circ f = \beta \circ f \circ \alpha$. The domains B and D from the complement division must be replaced by the family of domains given by the fibres of the projections. Thus, for each $a \in A$, the domain $B_a \cong \alpha^{-1}\{a\}$, and for each $c \in C$, the domain $D_c \cong \beta^{-1}\{c\}$. The function f may be regarded as a function $f : \sum(A, B) \to \sum(C, D)$[1]. By the isomorphism given in Chapter 5, we can also regard it to be $f : \prod(A, B \to \sum(C, D))$. By assumption, the value of C does not depend on B, so we may also regard f as a function $f : \prod(A, \sum(C, B \to D))$. Now the types of both the domain and the range of the residual version of f depend on the actual static value supplied.

An example will be useful. Suppose that f is a function $f : Union \to Union$ (using the type defined in Section 4.7) and that $f^{\#} \; TAG = TAG$. That is, in order to compute the tag of the result it is sufficient to know the tag of the argument. Furthermore, suppose that the tag of the argument is static, and so will be available during partial evaluation. The residual versions of f will all be tagless in both argument and result, and instead will map, say, characters to integers etc. Each will have a type appropriate to the (now absent) static tags. We can take this example further. Imagine an interpreter for a statically typed language which uses a universal value domain for the value of expressions. Suppose it is given sufficient static data for the value tags to be static. Then, instead of having to manipulate values in a universal type, the residual programs would manipulate data objects directly.

8.2.3 Self-Application

It is very noticeable that all the self-applicable partial evaluators to date have used S-expressions as their sole data structure. There are two reasons for this. Firstly, it is

---

[1]The notation $\sum(A, B)$ is short for $\sum_{a \in A} B_a$, and similarly for $\prod$.

very easy to represent programs using S-expressions, especially in LISP-like languages. More importantly, however, the absence of multiple types in the language means that a level of data encoding is not required. In Chapter 1, the type of *mix* was given as,

$$mix : \overline{A \times B \to C} \times \overline{A} \to \overline{B \to C}$$

and unless we have dependent types we can do no better. However, in the world of S-expressions, where there is a single universal type, the static input may be passed directly. Thus,

$$mix : \overline{A \times B \to C} \times A \to \overline{B \to C}$$

When this is applied to itself, we obtain the type of $mix_{\overline{mix}}$, namely

$$mix_{\overline{mix}} : \overline{A \times B \to C} \to \overline{A \to \overline{B \to C}}$$

This issue is considered in [Bon88] in the context of term rewriting systems with many signatures. Eventually, in order to produce a self-applicable partial evaluator, a single signature system was adopted.

Without a doubt, typed languages are here to stay, so a solution to this coding problem needs to be found if self-applicable partial evaluators are ever to be written in such languages. One possible method is to make the coding both as cheap as possible, and eliminable during partial evaluation. We can illustrate the former requirement as follows. Both of the (LISP style) expressions

        (cons (quote a) (cons (quote b) (quote nil)))
and
        (quote (a b))

evaluate to the list (a b), but the former entails a linear increase in size, whereas the latter only entails a constant increase. This difference becomes much greater if each expression is itself represented in the same manner. Using the first method, the size of the representation is exponential with respect to the representation level, whereas the second is linear. In a multiply typed language, therefore, some equivalent to quote must be included in the datatype representing expressions. This will, at least, prevent the self-applicable partial evaluator from requiring huge data structures.

8.2.4   Value Preservation

The binding-time analysis given in this thesis is not sufficiently strong to be adequate in every case. What is worse, it fails in one of the very cases where we would want it to succeed, that of interpreters which implement denotation semantics directly. An example, due to Mogensen, of the failure may be seen in interpreters for languages that handle state. The standard denotational description of such languages typically contains a function,

$$C : Com \rightarrow State \rightarrow State$$

(ignoring any environment parameter) where the state may be represented by an association list as usual. We will focus on two standard clauses in such a definition.

$$\mathcal{C}[\![\,C_1;C_2\,]\!]\sigma \;\;=\;\; \mathcal{C}[\![\,C_2\,]\!](\mathcal{C}[\![\,C_1\,]\!]\sigma)$$
$$\mathcal{C}[\![\,\text{if } E\ C_1\ C_2\,]\!]\sigma \;=\;\; \mathcal{E}[\![\,E\,]\!]\sigma \rightarrow \mathcal{C}[\![\,C_1\,]\!]\sigma,\ \mathcal{C}[\![\,C_2\,]\!]\sigma$$

The first expresses composition. The command function C returns the state resulting from the commands executed. The original state is given to the commands in C_1 and the state produced by these is given to C_2. The result is the final state after C_2 has effected any changes. The second equation handles if statements. The expression is evaluated in the current state and, depending on whether the result is *true* or *false*, the respective commands are executed with the current state. The result is the state after these commands have been performed.

In the standard scenario, the names in the state will be known during partial evaluation, but the values will not be available until run time. As a consequence, the result of $\mathcal{E}$ will be dynamic, but because of this, the state resulting from the execution of an if statement will be completely dynamic: the current binding-time analysis equations do not allow for the possibility for a dynamic conditional producing anything static. However, assuming a sensible block approach to introducing variables, the variable names *can* be determined during partial evaluation (if variables are introduced arbitrarily, then the name list may not be statically determined, of course).

In most cases it is quite correct that the result of an if with a dynamic condition should be dynamic. Even if both branches return completely static results, we will not be able to decide which static result will be the result of the if. There is one case, however, when we can determine it: when the static parts of the two branches are identical. Until a binding-time analysis is produced which captures this sort of static information, partial evaluation will not be able to produce compilers from some denotational style interpreters. This explains why we needed to adopt an unusual structure for the interpreter appearing in the extended example.

8.2.5 Domain Reduction

There is an additional optimisation that fits neatly into the framework we have constructed. Suppose that, by using projection-based strictness analysis, we discover that $f \circ \beta = f$ for some projection β. This means that we need no more that β's worth of information about the argument to f to be able to determine its result. So, rather than consider f to be a function $X \to Y$, say, we can regard it as a function $\beta(\!(X)\!) \to Y$. Then, when we factorise the domain of f's argument into static and dynamic parts, we start with a smaller domain than would otherwise be the case. Consequently, the residual functions may also end up with smaller argument domains.

The *length* function provides an example of this. Suppose that only the spine of a list is available during partial evaluation and that, for some reason, we wanted to produce a residual version of the *length* function. If the property that *length* = *length* $\circ$ *map ABS* was available to the partial evaluator then no run time arguments need to be produced. This possible optimisation is the natural extension of the notion of projection difference suggested in [Lau88].

8.3   Final Remarks

In this chapter we have seen some areas in which significant development of partial evaluation is still needed. Nonetheless, partial evaluation already is an exciting and promising method for both optimising interpretive programs, and for understanding the theoretical relationship between interpreters and compilers. To be generally useful in either of these areas, it is essential that its mathematical underpinnings are well developed. This is where the effort of this thesis has been directed. We hope that the results will be as useful in the long run as the excellent practical work of others has already proved to be.

Appendix A

Implementation of PEL

The projection-based partial evaluator described in this thesis was implemented in LML [Aug84]. The complete program is listed in these appendices for reference, together with some annotations intended to facilitate understanding. A complete listing of the extended example is given in Appendix C.

LML has an elementary module mechanism which was used to provide some structure to the program. The modules are presented more-or-less in dependency order, except that the general library functions appear in Appendix D.

A.1 Type Declarations

The important types used throughout the program are defined together. Two are used in the implementation of PEL itself, and two in binding-time analysis.

```
module  -- TYPES.M
export  term,domain,projection,sum;
```

The types `term` and `domain` provide representations for PEL-expressions and PEL-types respectively. The Bot summand of `term` is used to represent ⊥ after a projection has been applied by the function `sigma` (Appendix C).

```
rec
type    term    = Constr (List Char) term
                + Case term (List ((List Char) # (term # term)))
                + Prod (List term)
```

116

```
                    + Parm (List Char)
                    + Call (List Char) term
                    + RCall (List Char) term
                    + Bot
and
type    domain  = DProd (List domain)
                    + DFunctor (List Char) (List domain)
                    + DParm (List Char)
```

Projections are represented by the types `projection` and `sum`. Separating the representation in this way allows the LML typechecker to provide additional checks on projection manipulation. This is discussed in Appendix B.

```
and
type    projection
                = PProd (List projection)
                    + PMu (List Char)
                         (List ((List Char) # sum))
                         (List projection)
                    + PRec (List Char)
                    + PParm (List Char)
and
type    sum     = PAbs
                    + PSum (List ((List Char) # projection))
end
```

A.2 The PEL Interpreter

Now the implementation of PEL itself. The following module contains an interpreter, a parser, and a printer. The interpreter is the most significant as regards partial evaluation, for it is this that will be modified to produce the partial evaluator.

```
module  -- PEL.M
#include "library.t"
#include "parselib.t"
#include "types.t"
-- #include "globals.t"  (a cyclic dependency)
import  program : List ((List Char) # (term # term));
```

```
export  eval, make_env,
        parse, prog, fn, exp, type_def, type_dec,
        print_prog, print_fn, print_exp,
        print_type_def, print_type_dec, print_type;
```

A parsed program has type [(string,(term,term))]. The string (list of characters) component contains the function names, the first term a (possibly nested) product of parameter names, and the second term the body of the function. The environment is an association list between strings and terms, and the result of evaluation is a term.

```
rec    eval env (Parm v)      = lookup env v
||     eval env (Prod exps)   = Prod (map (eval env) exps)
||     eval env (Constr c arg) = Constr c (eval env arg)
||     eval env (Call f arg)   = let  (vs, body) = lookup program f in
                                      eval (make_env vs (eval env arg)) body
||     eval env (Case e cls)   = eval_case env (eval env e) cls

and    eval_case env (Constr name e_arg) ((c,(vs,exp)).cls)
          = if    name = c
            then  eval (make_env vs e_arg @ env) exp
            else  eval_case env (Constr name e_arg) cls

and    make_env (Parm x)     e     = [(x,e)]
||     make_env (Prod vs) (Prod es) = conc (map2 make_env vs es)
```

Parsing is split up into two phases, lexical and syntactic analysis. Lexemes are just strings. The only purpose of the lexer is to remove white space and to divide contiguous characters appropriately. The definitions of the basic parsing operators are given in Appendix D.

```
and    white   = some (sat (\c.c<=' '))
and    comment = lit '-' .. lit '-' .. skip '\n'
and    opchar  = sat (member "^-=|+>:")
and    identch = sat isupper !! sat islower !!
                 sat isdigit !! lit '_'

and    lexeme  = (white   .as. (\c.""))
                 !! (comment .as. (\c.""))
```

```
                    !! (sat (member "(),;[]#") .as. (\c.[c]))
                    !! (some opchar)
                    !! (sat isupper .. many identch .as. cons)
                    !! (sat islower   .. many identch .as. cons)
                    !! (some (sat isdigit))

and      lex inp = filter (\s.s~=[]) (fst (hd (many lexeme inp)))
and      parse p = hd o p o lex
```

The parser culminates in the function `prog` which, when applied to a program text, returns the parse tree. The tree has the structure

   `([type definition], ([(type declaration, function definition)], (term, type)))`

We allow the usual syntax for lists and numbers. However this is merely syntactic sugar for expressions such as `Cons (x,Nil)` or `Succ Zero` etc. The usual definitions of these types need to be provided for a program that uses these syntactic forms to be legal.

In the definition of the `prog` parser, the final expression may be optionally omitted. This is allowed merely in order to ensure that the parser is able to succeed if it hits a syntax error within a function definition.

```
and      prog  =   many type_def
                   .. many (type_dec .. fn)
                   .. opt (exp .. lit "::" x.. type_arg) (Prod [],DProd [])


and      fn    = lower .. patt .. lit "=" x.. exp ..x lit ";"


and      exp   = case_exp !! data !! call !! rcall !! simple


and      patt  = (lower  .as.  Parm) !!
                 (tuple patt  .as.  make Prod)
and      case_exp=   lit "case" x.. exp
                   .. lit "in"   x.. (clause .sep_by. lit "||")
                   ..x lit "end"          .as.  uncurry Case
and      clause = upper .. opt patt (Prod []) .. lit "->" x.. exp
and      data   = upper .. opt simple (Prod [])
                                  .as.  uncurry Constr
and      call   = lower .. simple  .as.  uncurry Call
and      rcall  = lit "#" x.. lower .. simple
```

```
                              .as. uncurry RCall
and     simple  = (parse_list exp .as. make_Cons)
             !! (lower   .as. Parm)
             !! (upper .as. (\c.Constr c (Prod [])))
             !! (tuple exp  .as.  make Prod)
             !! (number .as. (make_Succ o stoi))


and     type_def  = lit "type" x.. upper .. many lower
                      .. lit "=" x.. type_rhs ..x lit ";"


and     type_rhs  = (upper .. opt type_simple (DProd []))
                   .sep_by. lit "+"


and     type_simple = (lower  .as. DParm)
             !! (upper .as. (\c. DFunctor c []))
             !! (tuple type_arg  .as.  make DProd)


and     type_arg   = (upper .. many type_simple .as. uncurry DFunctor)
             !!  type_simple


and     type_dec= lower .. lit "::" x.. type_arg
                      .. lit "->" x.. type_arg ..x lit ";"


and     tuple p =  (lit "(" .. lit ")"  .as.  (\x.[]))
             !! (lit "(" x.. (p .sep_by. lit ",") ..x lit ")")


and     parse_list p =  (lit "[" .. lit "]" .as. \x.[])
                  !! (lit "[" x.. (p .sep_by. lit ",") ..x lit "]")


and     upper   = sat (\w. isupper (hd w))
and     lower   = sat (\w.islower (hd w) &
                   ~member ["case";"in";"end";"type"] w)
and     number  = sat (\w. isdigit (hd w))


and     make_Cons [] = Constr "Nil" (Prod [])
||      make_Cons (x.xs) = Constr "Cons" (Prod [x; make_Cons xs])


and     make_Succ 0 = Constr "Zero" (Prod [])
||      make_Succ n = Constr "Succ" (make_Succ (n-1))
```

The converse of a parser is a `print` function. Those defined here constitute an extremely basic pretty-printer, but the output is parseable by the parsers given above.

```
and     print_prog (tdefs,(tfs,(e,t)))
            = map_sep print_type_def "\n\n" tdefs @ "\n\n\n"
              @ map_sep print_tfs "\n\n" tfs @ "\n\n\n"
              @ print_exp e @ " :: " @ print_type t @ "\n\n"


and     print_fn (f,(x,exp)) = f @ print_arg x @ " =\n\t   "
                                @ print_exp exp @ ";"


and     print_exp (Case exp cls)
                = "case " @ print_exp exp @ " in\n\t    "
                    @ map_sep print_cl "\n\t||   " cls
                  @ "\n\tend"
||      print_exp (Constr name arg) = name @ print_carg arg
||      print_exp (Call name arg)   = name @ print_arg arg
||      print_exp (RCall name arg)  = "#" @ name @ print_arg arg
||      print_exp (Parm x)          = x
||      print_exp (Prod exps)       = "(" @ map_sep print_exp ", " exps @ ")"


and     print_arg (Parm x)     = " " @ x
||      print_arg (Prod exps)  = " (" @ map_sep print_exp ", " exps @ ")"
||      print_arg    any       = " (" @ print_exp any @ ")"


and     print_carg (Prod [])   = ""
||      print_carg  other      = print_arg other


and     print_cl (c,(x,e)) = c @ print_carg x @ " -> " @ print_exp e



and     print_type_def (f, (vs, cds))
                = "type " @ f @ " " @ map_sep id " " vs @ " =\n\t    "
                    @ map_sep print_summand "\n\t+ " cds @ ";"
and     print_summand (c,DProd []) = c
||      print_summand (c,t)        = c @ print_type_arg t


and     print_type (DParm x)      = x
||      print_type (DFunctor f ts) = f @ concmap print_type_arg ts
```

```
||      print_type (DProd xs)      = "(" @ map_sep print_type ", " xs @ ")"

and     print_type_arg (DParm x)  = " " @ x
||      print_type_arg (DProd ts) = " (" @ map_sep print_type ", " ts @ ")"
||      print_type_arg    any     = " (" @ print_type any @ ")"


and     print_tfs (t,fn) = print_type_dec t @ "\n" @ print_fn fn
and     print_type_dec (f,(t,s))= f @ " :: " @ print_type t
                                    @ " -> " @ print_type s @ ";"
end
```

A.3   Typechecking

PEL is a typed language. The implementation of typechecking follows. This may
be thought to be superfluous in an experimental system but in practice it has been
extremely useful in tracing errors in example programs. The typechecking module
makes heavy use of the YN datatype defined in the library module (Appendix D).
Use of this datatype makes failure (with messages) easy to propagate through the
use of the ~~~ operator. If the left hand argument fails, then the result is failure. If
it succeeds, then the right hand argument (a function) is applied to the successful
value.

```
module  -- CHECK.M
#include "library.t"
#include "types.t"
#include "pel.t"
-- #include "globals.t" (a cyclic dependency)
import  types : List ((List Char) # (domain # domain));

export  check_fn,check,app_type,unify;

rec     check_fn (f,(vs,e))
            = (f, lookupYN types f              ~~~ (\ (r,s).
                make_envYN vs r                 ~~~ (\ env.
                check false env e vars          ~~~ (\ (v,t,ns).
                unify v (DProd [app_type v r;t],
```

```
                       DProd [r;s])                ~~~ (\ u.
                 if    (app_type u s ~= s | app_type u r ~= r)
                 then  N "type too unconstrained"
                 else  Y []) ))))
```

The check function returns the type of the expression being checked, together with
a substitution function for the polymorphic variables (app_type is used to apply
substitutions). Due to the need for fresh variables a list of variables is piped around
the functions. The other parameters to check are: a boolean which determines
whether the expression may contain free variables (this is the means for indicating
absent data in the final expression); and an environment binding variables to their
types.

```
and     check b env (Parm x) (n.ns)
          = if    b
            then  Y (DParm, DParm n, ns)
            else  lookupYN env x  ~~~  \t. Y (DParm,t,ns)
||      check b env (Constr c e) ns
          = check b env e ns  ~~~  \(v,t,ns). apply_fnc c v t ns
||      check b env (Call f e) ns
          = check b env e ns  ~~~  \(v,t,ns). apply_fnc f v t ns
||      check b env (RCall f e) ns
          = check b env e ns  ~~~  \(v,t,ns). apply_fnc f v t ns
||      check b env (Prod es) ns
          = check_list b env es ns  ~~~  \(v,ts,ns). Y (v,DProd ts,ns)
||      check b env (Case e cls) ns
          = check b env e ns  ~~~  \(v,t,ns). check_cls b env v t cls ns


and     check_cls b env v t   []    (n.ns) = Y (v, DParm n, ns)
||      check_cls b env v t ((c,(vs,e)).cls) ns
          = check_cls b env v t cls ns              ~~~ (\ (v',u,ns).
            fresh_type c ns                         ~~~ (\ (r,s,ns).
            unify v' (s,t)                          ~~~ (\ w.
            make_envYN vs (app_type w r)            ~~~ (\ env'.
            check b (env' @ app_env w env) e ns ~~~ (\ (w',t,ns).
            Y (compose w' w, t, ns)                         )))))


and     check_list b env   []    ns = Y (DParm, [], ns)
||      check_list b env (e.es) ns
          = check b env e ns                        ~~~ (\ (v,t,ns).
```

```
                check_list b (app_env v env) es ns  ˜˜˜ (\ (u,ts,ns).
                Y (compose u v, (app_type u t).ts, ns)  ))


and     apply_fnc f v t ns = fresh_type f ns     ˜˜˜ (\ (r,s,ns).
                            unify v (r,t)        ˜˜˜ (\ w.
                        Y (w, app_type w s, ns) ))
```

Polymorphic type-checking requires unification. A fairly standard implementation
is given in the function `unify`. The first parameter to `unify` is a substitution, the
second is a pair of types to be unified.

```
and     unify v (DParm x, t) = if v x = DParm x
                                then  extend v x (app_type v t)
                                else  unify v (v x, app_type v t)
||      unify v (t, DParm x) = unify v (DParm x, t)
||      unify v (DFunctor f xs, DFunctor g ys)
            = if     f=g
              then   unify_list v (xs // ys)
              else   N ("Cannot unify " @ f @ " with " @ g)
||      unify v (DProd ds, DProd es)
            = if     length ds = length es
              then   unify_list v (ds // es)
              else   N "Cannot unify different size products"
||      unify v (s,t) = N ("Cannot unify " @ print_type s
                              @ " with " @ print_type t)


and     unify_list v    []      = Y v
||      unify_list v ((s,t).sts) = unify v (s,t) ˜˜˜ (\u. unify_list u sts)
```

The auxiliary functions required by the functions above appear next and are all fairly
self-explanatory. Some manipulate type variables and others manipulate program
variables.

```
and     free_vars (DParm y)      = [y]
||      free_vars (DProd ds)      = concmap free_vars ds
||      free_vars (DFunctor f ds) = concmap free_vars ds


and     fresh_type f ns = lookupYN types f ˜˜˜
                            (\ (r,s).
                                let rec  vr = free_vars r
```

```
                       and       vs = free_vars s
                       and       ns' = tail (length vr) ns
                       and       ns''= tail (length vs) ns'
                       and       env = (vr // ns) @ (vs // ns')
                    in  Y (subst env r, subst env s, ns'') )


and     subst env (DParm x)      = DParm (lookup env x)
||      subst env (DProd ds)     = DProd (map (subst env) ds)
||      subst env (DFunctor f ds) = DFunctor f (map (subst env) ds)


and     extend v x t = if t = DParm x then  Y v
                      else if    member (free_vars t) x
                        then  N ("Cyclic type: " @ x @ ", " @ print_type t)
                        else  Y (\y.if x=y then t else (v y))


and     app_type v (DParm y)      = v y
||      app_type v (DProd ds)     = DProd (map (app_type v) ds)
||      app_type v (DFunctor f ds) = DFunctor f (map (app_type v) ds)


and     app_env v env = map (\(x,y).(x, app_type v y)) env


and     compose v w x = app_type v (w x)


and     make_envYN (Parm x)  t  = Y [(x,t)]
||      make_envYN (Prod xs) (DProd ts)
                         = if  length xs = length ts
                           then  AppendYN (map2 make_envYN xs ts)
                           else  N "Cannot make environment to match"
||      make_envYN  any   any'  = N "Cannot make environment to match"
end
```

A.4 Global Values

Many items, such as the input program, remain unchanged throughout any particular execution and so are defined as global values. These values are defined on the
assumption that there are no errors, but if errors occur, the **result** function reports

those errors rather than returning a result that would require the other global values
to be evaluated.

```
module   -- GLOBALS.M
#include <OK>
#include <FILE>
#include "library.t"
#include "types.t"
#include "pel.t"
#include "check.t"


export   errm,unparsed,ill_typed,parsed_prog,
         type_defs,type_decs,program,
         expr,t_expr,types,
         result,
         cycles,mutual;
```

The value argv is a list of strings which gives the arguments supplied in the program
invocation. This list should contain the name of a file containing the input program.
Assuming such a file exists, the value of prog_text is the file's contents.

```
rec      (errm,prog_text) =
                   if argv=[] then
                     ("Please supply a file name",[])
                   else
                     case openfile (hd argv) in
                       Yes file: ([], file)
||                     No mesg : ("No file " @ hd argv @ "\n" @ mesg,[])
                     end
```

If prog_text represents a syntactically correct program, then the parser will reach
the end of the text resulting in an empty unparsed portion. In this case, the parsed
program may be split into its various components: type definitions, declarations giving the types of the functions defined in the program, function definitions, and a final
expression together with its type. The constant types is an association list giving
the declared types of all the functions and constructors defined in the program. The
function mutual takes a type name and returns the names of all the types mutually
recursive with with it. This uses the function cyclic (defined in Appendix D) which
takes a graph and returns an ordered list of its strongly connected components.

```
and     (parsed_prog,unparsed) = parse prog prog_text
and     (type_defs, (tf_defs,(expr,t_expr))) = parsed_prog
and     (type_decs, program) = unzip tf_defs

and     get_constr_types (t, (vs, cds))
           = [(c,(d, DFunctor t (map DParm vs)));; (c,d) <- cds]
and     types = type_decs @ concmap get_constr_types type_defs

and     cycles = cyclic (concmap edges type_defs) (map fst type_defs)
and     mutual x = hd [xs ;; xs<-cycles; member xs x]

and     edges (t,(vs,cds))
           = map (\f.(t,f)) (merge_list [functors d;; (c,d) <- cds])

and     functors (DProd ds)       = merge_list (map functors ds)
||      functors (DParm x)        = []
||      functors (DFunctor f ds) = merge_list ([f] . map functors ds)
```

If any errors arise then `errors` returns the appropriate message, otherwise it returns the empty string. The boolean argument allows for free variables to occur in the final expression. The function `result` returns its second argument only if no errors arise.

```
and     err_str (f, Y x)  = ""
||      err_str (f, N ms) = "\t" @ f @ ": " @ ms @ "\n"
and     ill_typed = concmap (err_str o check_fn) program

and     errors b
        = if  errm ~= []  then  errm

           else if  unparsed ~= []  then
             "Syntax error(s) in:\n" @ map_sep id " " unparsed

           else if  ill_typed ~= []  then
             "Error(s) in:\n" @ ill_typed

           else
             case  check b [] expr vars in
                 N ms : "Error(s) in final expression:\n\t" @ ms
             ||  Y x  : ""
             end
```

```
and      result b str1 str2 = str1 @ "\n\n"
                              @ case  errors b  in
                                    ""  : str2
                                || err : err
                                end
                              @ "\n\n"
end
```

A.5   The RUN Command

Finally, the run module collates all the previous into a single expression. When
compiled this produces a binary file which may be executed like any UNIX command.

```
--       RUN.M
#include "types.t"
#include "pel.t"
#include "globals.t"

         result false
         "Standard Interpretation of PEL"

         (print_exp (eval [] expr))
```

Appendix B

Implementation of BTA

This appendix contains the implementation of polymorphic projection-based binding-time analysis. The first module provides functions that manipulate the data structures used to represent projections; the second computes the abstract function environment $\phi^\#$ described in Chapter 4. The final executable file prints the result of the binding-time analysis.

B.1   Manipulating Projections

```
module  -- PROJECTIONS.M
#include "library.t"
#include "types.t"
#include "pel.t"
#include "globals.t"
-- #include "fn_vals.t" (a cyclic dependency)
import  fn_values: List ( ((List Char) # projection) # projection);
import  initial_env: List ( (List Char) # projection);

export  glb, glb_list, get_id, get_abs, make_abs,
        unfold, fold, extract, mask,
        get_env, squash, psubst,
        print_proj,print_proj_sum,
        evalp, make_penv, apply,
        descr, abs_env, description,iter_descr,descr;
```

The function `glb` computes the greatest lower bound of two projections while remaining within the finite domain. Its definition relies heavily on the fact that it will only ever be applied to projections defined over exactly the same type, and hence of the same structural form. Thus, in the various clauses below, we can guarantee that the names `f` and `g` are the same, for example.

```
rec     glb (PProd ps) (PProd qs) = PProd (map2 glb ps qs)
||      glb (PMu f fps ps) (PMu g gqs qs)
            = PMu f (map2 (\(h,p).\(k,q).(h, glbSum p q)) fps gqs)
                    (map2 glb ps qs)
||      glb (PRec f) (PRec g)     = PRec f
||      glb  any     (PParm y)    = any
||      glb (PParm x)   any       = any


and     glb_list (p.ps) = reduce glb p ps


and     glbSum   PAbs        p       = PAbs
||      glbSum    p         PAbs     = PAbs
||      glbSum (PSum cps) (PSum dqs) = let    (cs,ps) = unzip cps
                                       and    (ds,qs) = unzip dqs
                                       in     PSum (cs // map2 glb ps qs)
```

In a number of different situations we need to produce either *ID* or *ABS* over particular types. These have a structural form which reflects the definition of the type. This insistence on retaining the appropriate structural form has many benefits during the manipulation of projections.

```
and     get_id t = get_id' [] t
and     get_id' ts (DProd ds) = PProd (map (get_id' ts) ds)
||      get_id' ts (DParm x)  = PParm x
||      get_id' ts (DFunctor f ds)
            = if member ts f then PRec f else
              let ts'=mutual f in
              PMu f [(t, PSum [(c, get_id' (ts@ts') d);; (c,d)<-cds]) ;;
                                    (t,(vs,cds))<-type_defs; member ts' t]
                  (map (get_id' ts) ds)


and     get_abs t = get_abs' [] t
and     get_abs' ts (DProd ds) = PProd (map (get_abs' ts) ds)
```

```
||      get_abs' ts (DParm x) = PParm x
||      get_abs' ts (DFunctor f ds)
            = if member ts f then PRec f else
              PMu f [(t,PAbs);; t <- mutual f] (map (get_abs' ts) ds)

and     make_abs (PProd ps)     = PProd (map make_abs ps)
||      make_abs (PParm x)      = PParm x
||      make_abs (PMu f fps ps)
            = PMu f [(f,PAbs);; (f,p) <- fps] (map make_abs ps)
```

In order to get "inside" a projection on a recursive type we must unfold the definition. This will involve substituting the original projection for the recursive markers, and substituting the appropriate projections for the polymorphic parameters. Notice that the result in a sum-type projection, thus allowing the type system to distinguish between a folded and unfolded projection.

In the definition of unfold_rec we may safely pass over PMu g gqs as, by assumption on the construction of the original projection argument to unfold, the type g is not in mutual recursion with f.

```
and     unfold (PMu f fps ps)
            = let (vs,cds) = lookup type_defs f
              in  case lookup fps f in
                      PAbs     : PAbs
||                    PSum cps : PSum
                                 [(c, unfold_rec (vs//ps) fps ps p);; (c,p) <- cps]
                  end

and     unfold_rec env fps ps p
            = case p in
                  PProd qs      : PProd (map (unfold_rec env fps ps) qs)
||                PMu g gqs qs  : PMu g gqs (map (unfold_rec env fps ps) qs)
||                PRec g        : PMu g fps ps
||                PParm x       : lookup env x
              end
```

The fold function is a converse to unfold. Its arguments represent the projection c_0 $ID + \cdots + c$ $p + \cdots + c_n$ ID as occurs in the constructor clause of the abstract semantics. This is not, in general, an unfolded version of a projection in the finite

domain (though, by assumption, all the projections it refers to are). Thus, in folding
the projection, some information will be lost, as evidenced by the call to `glb_list`.

In `extract`, the `ts` parameter is a list of all the types whose definitions are in mutual
recursion with `f`.

```
and     fold c p
          = let rec  (r,DFunctor f ds) = lookup types c
              and        ts = mutual f
              and        (rp, env) = (squash r p, get_env r p)
              in      glb_list (mask ts c env rp . extract ts f rp)


and     extract ts f (PProd ps) = conc (map (extract ts f) ps)
||      extract ts f (PMu g gps ps)
          = if member ts g then [PMu f gps ps] else
                conc (map (extract ts f) ps)
||      extract ts f (PRec g)   = []
||      extract ts f (PParm x)  = []


and     mask ts c env p = let rec  (r,s) = lookup types c
                            and        (PMu f fps ps) = get_id s
                            in    PMu f [(f, insert ts c p q);; (f,q) <- fps]
                                        (map (instance env) ps)


and     insert ts c p PAbs = PAbs
||      insert ts c p (PSum cps)
          = PSum [if c=c' then  (c, ins ts p) else  (c',q);; (c',q) <- cps]


and     ins ts (PProd ps)      = PProd (map (ins ts) ps)
||      ins ts (PParm x)       = PParm x
||      ins ts (PMu f fps ps) = if member ts f then  PRec f else
                                    PMu f fps (map (ins ts) ps)


and     instance env (PParm x) = lookup' (PParm x) env x
```

To implement the material of Chapter 7, we have to be able to factorise a projection into its polymorphic and monomorphic parts. This factorisation is not always
exact as it may involve taking the glb of different projections that appear in the
position of multiple occurrences of a single type variable. The function `squash` takes
a type that may involve free type variables, together with a projection over an in-

stance of the type, and returns the corresponding projection over the original type.
In contrast `get_env` extracts the parts of the projection occurring at each polymorphic point and constructs an environment binding the type variables to their
respective projections. Constructing the environment may involve approximation if
a single type variable appears more than once. The "inverse" to these is `psubst`
which takes a polymorphic projection, together with an environment binding type
variables to projections, and substitutes for these variables in the projection. Thus
`psubst (get_env r p) (squash r p)` $\sqsubseteq$ p for all types r and projections p.

```
and     squash (DProd ds) (PProd ps)          = PProd (map2 squash ds ps)
||      squash (DParm x)     p                 = PParm x
||      squash    d          (PParm x)         = get_id d
||      squash (DFunctor f ds) (PMu g gps ps)  = PMu g gps (map2 squash ds ps)


and     get_env (DProd ds) (PProd ps) = join_list glb (map2 get_env ds ps)
||      get_env (DParm x)    p         = [(x,p)]
||      get_env (DFunctor f ds) (PMu g gps ps)
                                       = join_list glb (map2 get_env ds ps)


and     psubst env (PProd ps)       = PProd (map (psubst env) ps)
||      psubst env (PParm x)        = lookup env x
||      psubst env (PMu f fps ps)   = PMu f fps (map (psubst env) ps)


and     abs_env c vs p
          = let  (r,s) = lookup types c in
             make_penv vs (psubst (get_env s (make_abs p)) (get_abs r))
```

The function `print_proj` provides a textual representation of projections.

```
and     print_proj (PProd ps) = "(" @ map_sep print_proj ", " ps @ ")"
||      print_proj (PRec f)    = "(PRec " @ show_string f @ ")"
||      print_proj (PParm x)   = x
||      print_proj (PMu f fps ps)
          = "(PMu " @ show_string f @ " "
               @ show_list (show_pair (show_string,print_proj_sum)) fps
               @ " " @ show_list print_proj ps @ ")"


and     print_proj_sum    PAbs      = "PAbs"
||      print_proj_sum (PSum cps)
          = "(PSum " @ show_list (show_pair (show_string,print_proj)) cps @ ")"
```

In Chapter 4 we presented the $\mathcal{E}^{\#}$ function. Here it is called `evalp`. It takes an environment associating parameter names with projections, and an expression, and returns the projection value of the expression. The function `evalp` has access to the complete abstract function environment through the use of `apply`. This function environment is computed in the module `fn_vals` (in this appendix).

```
and     evalp env (Parm v)       = lookup env v
||      evalp env (Prod es)       = PProd (map (evalp env) es)
||      evalp env (Constr c e)    = fold c (evalp env e)
||      evalp env (Call f e)      = apply f (evalp env e)
||      evalp env (RCall f e)     = applyR f (evalp env e)
||      evalp env (Case e cls)
          = let  p = evalp env e  in
              case unfold p in
                PAbs : let (c,(vs,e))=hd cls in
                    make_abs (evalp (abs_env c vs p @ env) e)
||              PSum cps : glb_list
                    [evalp (make_penv vs (lookup cps c) @ env) e;; (c,(vs,e)) <- cls]
              end

and     make_penv (Parm x)     p       = [(x,p)]
||      make_penv (Prod vs) (PProd ps) = conc (map2 make_penv vs ps)

and     apply f p = let  (r,s) = lookup types f
                    in   psubst (get_env r p) (lookup fn_values (f,squash r p))

and     applyR f p = let  (r,s) = lookup types f
                     in   psubst (get_env r (make_abs p)) (get_abs s)
```

In addition to implementing $\mathcal{E}^{\#}$, we must implement $\mathcal{P}^{\#}$. This also takes an abstract environment and an expression, but returns a list of function names paired with projections which (in the limit—see below) places lower bounds on the amount of information available to each function at partial evaluation time. The value `description` is the final result of the binding-time analysis and corresponds to the result of $\mathcal{M}^{\#}$.

```
and     descr env (Parm v)       = []
||      descr env (Prod es)       = join_list glb (map (descr env) es)
||      descr env (Constr c e)    = descr env e
||      descr env (Call f e)      = let (r,s) = lookup types f in
```

```
                       join glb [(f, squash r (evalp env e))] (descr env e)
||      descr env (RCall f e)  = let (r,s) = lookup types f in
                       join glb [(f, squash r (evalp env e))] (descr env e)
||      descr env (Case e cls) = let  p = evalp env e  in
             join glb (descr env e)
             (case unfold p in
               PAbs : join_list glb
                  [descr (abs_env c vs p @ env) e;; (c,(vs,e)) <- cls]
||             PSum cps : join_list glb
                              [descr (make_penv vs (lookup cps c) @ env) e;;
                                 (c,(vs,e)) <- cls]
          end)

and     iter_descr desc = join glb desc (join_list glb (map descr_fn desc))
and     descr_fn (f,p) = let  (vs,body) = lookup program f in
                           descr (make_penv vs p) body

and     description = limit (repeat iter_descr (descr initial_env expr))
end
```

B.2   The Abstract Function Environment

The abstract function environment $\phi^{\#}$ (Chapter 4) is computed by the functions in this module. Its value is given by the constant **fn_values**, which is defined by iteration to the greatest fixed point. Rather than compute the whole of $\phi^{\#}$ (it is, in general, exceedingly expensive to do so), we compute only the portion that may actually be required. As described in Chapter 6, we use a table to describe this minimal portion of $\phi^{\#}$, hence the name *minimal function graph*.

The table has the structure [((function name, argument),result)]. We begin with an initial table extracted from the expression at the end of the program. This table defines which calls of which abstract functions we are initially interested in. As we know nothing about the results of applying the abstract functions at this stage, we pair these calls with *ID* as an (over-)approximation to their results. The function **iter_fns** applies the abstract evaluator to each element of the table to produce a more accurate approximation. In the process the abstract evaluator uses the current table to provide results of any function calls it needs to evaluate. Any function/argument pairs whose result is needed by the evaluator but not *explicitly* represented in the table are returned by the evaluator for inclusion in the table on the next iteration.

When the application of `iter_fns` to the table produces the same table as a result, a fixed point will have been reached (the argument/result pairs in the table are correct and no new components were required), and the process terminates.

```
module  -- FN_VALS.M
#include "library.t"
#include "types.t"
#include "pel.t"
#include "check.t"
#include "globals.t"
#include "projections.t"


export  fn_values, iter_fns, initial_table, initial_env,
        evalf, apply_fn;


rec     fn_values = limit (repeat iter_fns initial_table)


and     iter_fns table
           = let   (table',tabs) = unzip (map (iter_fn table) table)
             in    join_list glb (table'.tabs)
and     iter_fn table ((f,p),q)
             = let rec   (vs,body) = lookup program f
                   and         (q',tab) = evalf table (make_penv vs p) body
                   in   ( ((f,p),q') , tab)
```

The initial table is obtained from the expression at the end of the program and contains the names of the functions appearing in the expression, together with a projection describing how much of their arguments are present. Any free variable give rise to the *ABS* projection, and actual values lead to non-*ABS* projections. From this point onwards, the only information that the binding-time analyser uses is the presence or absence of data, and not the values themselves. Hence, the bulk of the binding-time analysis presented here is actually metastatic. If the initial table was provided independently as an annotation then the whole of binding-time analysis would indeed be metastatic.

```
and     initial_table = snd (evalf [] initial_env expr)
and     initial_env   = get_abs_env expr t_expr
```

```
and     get_abs_env (Parm x)     t       = [(x, get_abs t)]
||      get_abs_env (Prod es) (DProd ds) = conc (map2 get_abs_env es ds)
||      get_abs_env (Call f e)   t       = get_abs_env e (arg_type f t)
||      get_abs_env (RCall f e)  t       = get_abs_env e (arg_type f t)
||      get_abs_env (Constr c e) t       = get_abs_env e (arg_type c t)

and     arg_type f t = let (r,s) = lookup types f in
                         case unify DParm (s,t) in
                           Y v : app_type v r
                         end
```

The evaluator returns a pair of values. The first is the abstract value of an expression computed with respect to the function table provided. The second is a table of all the (possibly new) function/argument pairs that were used, paired with the best approximation to the result then known. This table is used to extend the function environment.

```
and     evalf vals env (Parm v)     = (lookup env v, [])
||      evalf vals env (Prod es)    = (PProd, join_list glb) @2
                                         unzip (map (evalf vals env) es)
||      evalf vals env (Constr c e) = (fold c, id) @2 evalf vals env e
||      evalf vals env (Call f e)   = apply_fn vals f (evalf vals env e)
||      evalf vals env (RCall f e)  = apply_fn vals f (evalf vals env e)
||      evalf vals env (Case e cls)
          = let    (p,t) = evalf vals env e in
            case unfold p in
              PAbs : let (c,(vs,e))=hd cls in
                        (make_abs,id) @2 (evalf vals (abs_env c vs p @ env) e)
||            PSum cps : let (ps,ts) = unzip
                             [evalf vals (make_penv vs (lookup cps c) @ env) e;;
                              (c,(vs,e)) <- cls] in
                           (glb_list ps, join_list glb (t.ts))
            end

and     apply_fn vals f (p,t)
          = let rec    (r,s) = lookup types f
               and     (q,env) = (squash r p, get_env r p)
               and     fq = apply_tab f q s vals
            in
               (psubst env fq, join glb [((f,q),fq)] t)
```

The table contains graphs of approximations of each of the functions (any function that is not called is given by the empty graph). The meaning of any particular function f is defined to be $f_{tab}\, x = \prod \{y \mid \exists z\,.\, x \sqsubseteq z,\ \{f : z \mapsto y\} \in tab\}$. The apparently simpler method of pairing new function/argument pairs with *ID* runs into theoretical difficulties, in that the table may for a time represent non-monotonic functions. In fact, the theoretical difficulties turn out not to cause problems, but the method we have used is both cleaner and, in general, requires fewer iterations to find the fixed point.

```
and     apply_tab f p s [] = get_id s
||      apply_tab f p s (((g,q),gq).rest)
          = if  f=g & less p q  then
                    glb gq (apply_tab f p s rest)
              else  apply_tab f p s rest


and     less (PParm x) (PParm y)   = true
||      less (PRec x)  (PRec y)    = true
||      less (PProd ps) (PProd qs) = And (map2 less ps qs)
||      less (PMu f fps ps) (PMu g gqs qs)
          =   And (map2 (\x.\y.less_sum (snd x) (snd y)) fps gqs)
            & And (map2 less ps qs)


and     less_sum PAbs any = true
||      less_sum any PAbs = false
||      less_sum (PSum cps) (PSum dqs)
          = And (map2 (\x.\y.less (snd x) (snd y)) cps dqs)
end
```

B.3   Binding-Time Analysis Output

We have not defined an intermediate annotated version of PEL designed to convey binding-time information as this is only actually *necessary* for self-application. Instead, the binding-time information is computed each time the program is specialised to some input values. However, if separate binding-time information is required it may be obtained from the following executable program.

```
--      BTA.M
#include "library.t"
#include "types.t"
#include "globals.t"
#include "projections.t"

let     sep = "\n\n=======================================\n\n"
and     pr (f,p) = f @ ":\n" @ print_proj p

in      result true
        "Projection-Based Partial Evaluation"

        ("Binding-Times Analysis Results:" @ sep
           @ map_sep pr "\n\n" description @ sep)
```

In Appendix C we discuss the way in which the specialiser uses the binding-time information computed by the modules occurring here.

Appendix C

Implementation of Specialisation

This appendix contains the definition of the specialiser itself. The module `spec.m` provides the definitions of the specialisation functions, and these are brought together at the end of the appendix into an executable program. The appendix closes with the example specialisation referred to in Section 7.5.

C.1   Specialisation

```
module  --      SPEC.M
#include "library.t"
#include "types.t"
#include "pel.t"
#include "globals.t"
#include "projections.t"
#include "fn_vals.t"

export  spec,resid_prog,sigma,delta,
        make_menv,self_env;
```

The key function in specialisation is `spec`. The first argument to `spec` is often called the *pending list*. It consists of a list of function names, each paired with a static value, that await specialisation. The second argument is also a list of function/static-value pairs corresponding to the specialisations already performed. Static values contain occurrences of `Bot` where the static projection has caused the dynamic value to be blotted out. Each of these occurrences is replaced with a fresh parameter name (obtained from the list vars), and a product of these new names is constructed by delta (corresponding to the δ function of Chapter 5). After the function body has been evaluated it is searched to find any function calls that will themselves need specialisation.

```
rec     spec   []     table  = []
||      spec (fn.fns) table
          = if  member table fn  then
                spec fns table
            else let
                rec     (f,arg)      = fn
                and     (vs, body)   = lookup program f
                and     (arg',vars') = replace arg vars
                and     new_vs       = delta arg arg'
                and     new_body     = evalm (make_menv vs arg') body
                and     new_fns      = search new_body
                in   (fn,(new_vs,new_body)) . spec (fns @ new_fns) (fn.table)

and     replace  Bot       (n.ns) = (Parm n, ns)
||      replace (Constr c e) ns = (Constr c, id) @2 replace e ns
||      replace (Prod es) ns     = (Prod, id) @2 feed replace es ns

and     evalm env (Parm x)       = lookup env x
||      evalm env (Prod exps)    = Prod (map (evalm env) exps)
||      evalm env (Constr c arg)= Constr c (evalm env arg)
||      evalm env (Call f arg)   = let  (vs, body) = lookup program f  in
                                        evalm (make_menv vs (evalm env arg)) body
||      evalm env (RCall f arg) = RCall f (evalm env arg)
||      evalm env (Case e cls)  = evalm_case env (evalm env e) cls

and     evalm_case env (Constr name e_arg) ((c,(vs,exp)).cls)
            = if name = c then  evalm (make_menv vs e_arg @ env) exp
                        else  evalm_case env (Constr name e_arg) cls
||      evalm_case env  any  cls
            = Case any [(c,(vs, evalm (self_env vs @ env) e));; (c,(vs,e)) <- cls]

and     self_env (Parm x)     = [(x,Parm x)]
||      self_env (Call f e)   = self_env e
||      self_env (RCall f e)  = self_env e
```

```
||      self_env (Constr c e) = self_env e
||      self_env (Prod es)    = concmap self_env es


and     make_menv (Parm x)      e    = [(x,e)]
||      make_menv (Prod vs) (Prod es) = conc (map2 make_menv vs es)
||      make_menv (Prod vs)      e    = conc (map (\y.make_menv y e) vs)
```

Projections are applied using **sigma**. Given a function name and an expression (assumed to be an argument to the function), **sigma** extracts from the binding-time description the projection associated with the function, and applies it to the expression. Because the recursion is guided by the projection, the parts of the expression reached will be in normal form. When the projection *ABS* is encountered the expression Bot is returned, representing $\perp$.

```
and     sigma f e = sigma_exp (lookup description f) e
and     sigma_exp (PProd ps) (Prod es) = Prod (map2 sigma_exp ps es)
||      sigma_exp (PMu f fps ps) e      = sigma_sum (unfold (PMu f fps ps)) e
||      sigma_exp (PParm x)       e     = Bot


and     sigma_sum    PAbs       e      = Bot
||      sigma_sum (PSum cps) (Constr c e) = Constr c (sigma_exp (lookup cps c) e)


and     delta e' e = make Prod (delta_exp e' e)
and     delta_exp    Bot          e      = [e]
||      delta_exp  (Prod es')    (Prod es)  = conc (map2 delta_exp es' es)
||      delta_exp (Constr c' e') (Constr c e) = delta_exp e' e


and     delta_type e' e = make DProd (delta_t e' e)
and     delta_t    Bot        t      = [t]
||      delta_t (Prod es) (DProd ts) = conc (map2 delta_t es ts)
||      delta_t (Constr c e) (DFunctor f ts)
            = let (vs,cds) = lookup type_defs f in
                  delta_t e (subst (vs//ts) (lookup cds c))


and     subst env (DParm x)       = lookup env x
||      subst env (DProd ds)      = DProd (map (subst env) ds)
||      subst env (DFunctor f ds) = DFunctor f (map (subst env) ds)
```

The function **search** will go through the specialised function body and pick out any remaining function calls along with the static part of the arguments. Repeats are not checked for, as they will not cause a problem for spec.

```
and      search (Parm x)      = []
||       search  Bot          = []
||       search (RCall f arg) = (f, sigma f arg) . search arg
||       search (Constr c arg) = search arg
||       search (Prod es)      = concmap search es
||       search (Case exp cls) = search exp @ conc [search e;; (c,(vs,e))<-cls]
```

Having produced the specialised program, we need to tidy it up by renaming each specialisation of the original functions. First a table is constructed of the instantiations giving the new name, and then the program is altered to suit. At this point the new types of the residual functions may be generated from the old using a version of delta defined over types.

```
and      rename_fn ns (fn,(vs,body))
            = let rec    new_f = lookup ns fn
              and        (f,e) = fn
              and        (r,s) = lookup types f  in
            ( (new_f, (delta_type e r, s)),
                (new_f, (vs, rename_exp ns body))  )
```

```
and      rename_exp ns (Parm x)      = Parm x
||       rename_exp ns  Bot          = Bot
||       rename_exp ns (Constr c e) = Constr c (rename_exp ns e)
||       rename_exp ns (Prod es)      = Prod (map (rename_exp ns) es)
||       rename_exp ns (RCall f e)
            = let  se = sigma f e  in
                Call (lookup ns (f,se)) (delta se (rename_exp ns e))
||       rename_exp ns (Case exp cls)
            = Case (rename_exp ns exp) [(c,(vs,rename_exp ns e));; (c,(vs,e))<-cls]
```

```
and      new_name n ((f,arg),rhs) = ((f,arg), f @ "_" @ n)
```

The functions above are now combined to give produce the residual program. The type definitions appearing in the residual program will be a subset of the definitions appearing in the original. The function get_types scans the (new) types of the residual functions and inserts the required type definitions.

```
and      get_types ts [] = []
```

```
||      get_types ts (((f,(r,s)),fn_def).rest)
          = let  t1 = difference (scan r) ts  in
            let  t2 = difference (scan s) (t1@ts) in
               [(t,def);; (t,def) <- type_defs; member (t1@t2) t]
                 @ get_types (t1@t2@ts) rest


and     scan (DProd ds) = merge_list (map scan ds)
||      scan (DParm x)  = []
||      scan (DFunctor f ds)
                        = merge_list ([[g];; g<- mutual f] @ map scan ds)


and     resid_prog
          = let rec  new_expr  = evalm (self_env expr) expr
            and      spec_fns  = spec (search new_expr) []
            and      new_names = map2 new_name vars spec_fns
            and      new_fns   = map (rename_fn new_names) spec_fns
            and      new_types = get_types [] new_fns
            in
               (new_types,
                (new_fns,
                 (rename_exp new_names new_expr, t_expr)))
end
```

C.2   Residual Program Output

All the modules used up to now are brought together by the following executable
which, when compiled, produces a UNIX command to perform partial evaluation.

```
--      PE.M
#include "types.t"
#include "pel.t"
#include "globals.t"
#include "spec.t"


let     sep = "\n\n========================================\n\n"


in      result true
```

```
"Projection-Based Partial Evaluation"

("Partially Evaluated Program:" @ sep @ print_prog resid_prog @ sep)
```

C.3 Extended Example

We conclude this appendix with an actual listing obtained from the partial evaluator. We specialise the imperative language interpreter introduced in Chapter 2 (given below) to the factorials program of Section 6.4. The definitions of functions such as gt (>) have been deleted as they do not affect the results—the residual versions are identical to the original versions.

```
type Command =   Read Ident
               + Write Exp
               + Alloc (Ident, List Command)
               + DeAlloc
               + Assign (Ident, Exp)
               + If (Exp, List Command, List Command)
               + While (Exp, List Command);

type Exp = Val Num + Id Ident + Op (Oper, Exp, Exp);
type Ident = X + Y + Z;
type Oper  = Gt + Mul + Minus;

type List a = Nil + Cons (a, List a);

type Num = Zero + Succ Num;


exec :: (List Command, List Num) -> List Num;
exec (block, inp) = run (block, Nil, inp);

run :: (List Command, List (Ident,Num), List Num) -> List Num;
run (block, env, inp)
      = case block in Nil -> Nil || Cons (com,coms) -> case com in
        Read k
           -> run (coms, update (env, k, #hd inp), #tl inp)
```

```
        || Write e
            -> Cons (eval (env,e), run (coms, env, inp))
        || Alloc (k,cs)
            -> run (append (cs, Cons (DeAlloc,coms)), Cons ((k,Zero),env), inp)
        || DeAlloc
            -> run (coms, tl env, inp)
        || Assign (k,e)
            -> run (coms, update (env, k, eval (env,e)), inp)
        || If (e, cs1, cs2)
            -> #if (eval (env,e), run (append (cs1,coms), env, inp),
                                  run (append (cs2,coms), env, inp))
        || While (e,cs)
            -> #run ([If (e, append (cs,block), coms)], env, inp)
        end
        end;


eval :: (List (Ident,Num), Exp) -> Num;
eval (env,e) = case e in
                  Val n -> n
              ||  Id k -> lookup (env,k)
              ||  Op (oper,e1,e2) ->
                      case oper in
                          Gt    -> #gt (eval (env,e1), eval (env,e2))
                      || Mul    -> #mul (eval (env,e1), eval (env,e2))
                      || Minus  -> #minus (eval (env,e1), eval (env,e2))
                      end
                  end;


lookup :: (List (Ident,Num), Ident) -> Num;
lookup (env,k) = case env in
                  Cons ((j,y),jys) -> if (eq (k,j), y, lookup (jys,k))
                  end;


update :: (List (Ident,Num), Ident, Num) -> List (Ident, Num);
update (env,k,v) = case env in
                      Cons ((j,y),jys)
                         -> if (eq (k,j), Cons ((j,v),jys),
                                          Cons ((j,y), update (jys,k,v)))
                      end;
```

```
eq :: (Ident,Ident) -> Num;
eq (j,k) =case j in
              X -> case k in X->1 || Y->0 || Z->0 end
           || Y -> case k in X->0 || Y->1 || Z->0 end
           || Z -> case k in X->0 || Y->0 || Z->1 end
          end;


if :: (Num,a,a) -> a;
if (n,x,y) = case n in Zero -> y || Succ m -> x end;

append :: (List a, List a) -> List a;
append (xs,ys) = case xs in
                  Nil -> ys
               || Cons (z,zs) -> Cons (z, append (zs,ys))
                  end;

hd :: List a -> a;
hd xs = case xs in Cons (y,ys) -> y end;

tl :: List a -> List a;
tl xs = case xs in Cons (y,ys) -> ys end;

gt :: (Num,Num) -> Num;
gt (n,m) = ... ;

mul :: (Num,Num) -> Num;
mul (n,m) = ... ;

minus :: (Num,Num) -> Num;
minus (n,m) = ... ;


#exec   ([ Alloc (X,
          [ Read X,
            While (Op (Gt, Id X, Val 0),
            [ Alloc (Y,
              [ Assign (Y, Val 1),
                While (Op (Gt, Id X, Val 0),
                [ Assign (Y, Op (Mul, Id Y, Id X)),
```

```
                    Assign (X, Op (Minus, Id X, Val 1)) ]),
                  Write (Id Y) ]),
                Read X ]),
              Write (Val 0) ]) ],


        input


    ) :: List Num
```

The result of specialisation is the following residual program. Apart from altering
the layout of the program (including sugaring the syntax of numbers and lists), and
deleting the definitions of functions such as gt (>), the output is unchanged. Note
in particular that different residual versions of run are equipped with distinct types.

```
Projection-Based Partial Evaluation


Partially Evaluated Program:


==========================================

type List a = Nil + Cons (a, List a);


type Num  = Zero + Succ (Num);



exec_a :: List (Num) -> List (Num);
exec_a a = run_b (hd_c a, tl_d a);


run_b :: (Num, List (Num)) -> List (Num);
run_b (a, b) = if_e (gt_f (a, 0), run_g (1, a, b), [0]);


run_g :: (Num, Num, List (Num)) -> List (Num);
run_g (a, b, c) = if_e (gt_f (b, 0),
                    run_g (mul_h (a, b), minus_i (b, 1), c),
                    Cons (a, run_b (hd_c c, tl_d c)));



hd_c :: List a -> a;
hd_c a = case a in Cons (y, ys) -> y end;
```

```
tl_d :: List a -> List a;
tl_d a = case a in Cons (y, ys) -> ys end;

if_e :: (Num, a, a) -> a;
if_e (a, b, c) = case a in
                      Zero -> c
                  ||  Succ m -> b
                  end;

gt_f :: (Num, Num) -> Num;
gt_f (a, b) = ... ;

mul_h :: (Num, Num) -> Num;
mul_h (a, b) = ... ;

minus_i :: (Num, Num) -> Num;
minus_i (a, b) = ... ;


exec_a input :: List (Num)

==========================================
```

Substituting any value for the free variable `input` in either the original or the residual program will give identical results, but with significantly less computation needed in the latter case.

Appendix D

Library Functions

D.1   General Library Functions

In addition to the standard prelude of LML the following functions were needed. Most of these are fairly familiar, but those that are less so will be explained.

```
module  -- LIBRARY.M
infixr  "//";   -- curried form of zip
infixr  "@2";  -- apply function on pairs
infixr  "~~~";  -- combinator for YN type

export  fst,snd,cons,uncurry,@2,id,//,unzip,
        lookup,lookup',member,
        map_sep,map2,feed,
        make,repeat,limit,vars,
        join,join_list,merge,merge_list,
        cyclic,dfs,span,
        YN,~~~,lookupYN,AppendYN,listYN;

rec     fst (x,y) = x
and     snd (x,y) = y
and     cons (x,xs) = x.xs
and     swap (x,y) = (y,x)
and     uncurry f (x,y) = f x y
and     (f,g) @2 (x,y) = (f x, g y)
and     id x = x
```

```
and        []  //  ys   = []
||         xs  //  []   = []
||         (x.xs) // (y.ys) = (x,y) . (xs // ys)


and        unzip      []      = ([],[])
||         unzip ((x,y).xys) = ((\xs.(x.xs)), (\ys.(y.ys))) @2 (unzip xys)


and        lookup      ((n,v).rest) m = if n=m then v else lookup rest m
and        lookup' def ((n,v).rest) m = if n=m then v else lookup' def rest m
||         lookup' def     []       m = def


and        member xs x = mem x xs
```

In addition to the usual `map` function, other variants are convenient. The function `map2` is a binary version of `map`, and `map_sep` concatenates the result list but inserts the separator provided. The `feed` function acts like map except that a second, state-like, parameter is fed down the list. This is used to pass a list of new variable names so that at each application the function `f` has access to fresh variables.

```
and        map2 f    []    ys   = []
||         map2 f    xs    []   = []
||         map2 f (x.xs) (y.ys) = f x y . map2 f xs ys


and        map_sep f str   []    = []
||         map_sep f str   [x]   = f x
||         map_sep f str (x.xs) = f x @ str @ map_sep f str xs


and        feed f    []   ns = ([], ns)
||         feed f (x.xs) ns = let (y, ns') = f x ns
                              in  ((\ys.y.ys), id) @2 feed f xs ns'
```

The main use of `make` is in conjunction with constructors such as `Prod` where the constructor is only required if the list is not a singleton. The function `repeat` generates an infinite list of iterations of its function argument, and `limit` extracts the element of the list once stability has been reached. The list `vars` is an infinte list of distinct variable names.

```
and        make c [x] = x
||         make c xs  = c xs
```

```
and     repeat f x = x . repeat f (f x)
and     limit (x.y.rest) = if x=y then x else limit (y.rest)

and     atoz  = "abcdefghijklmnopqrstuvwxyz"
and     vars  = [[x];; x <- atoz] @ [(x.xs);; xs <- vars; x <- atoz]
```

The merge function merges ordered lists. Similarly, the join function is used to merge ordered association lists. When the names p and q are distinct the action is clear, but when they are the same their values are combined. As the method of combination depends on the situation we use an extra parameter to describe it. Note that in general the "names" p and q might be fairly large objects, representations of projections for example. The ordering is the built in LML total ordering provided over all algebraic datatypes.

```
and     merge   []      ys    = ys
||      merge   xs      []    = xs
||      merge (x.xs) (y.ys) = if x<y then  x . merge xs (y.ys)  else
                              if x>y then  y . merge (x.xs) ys  else
                                           x . merge xs ys

and     merge_list = reduce merge []

and     join f     xs      []    = xs
||      join f     []      ys    = ys
||      join f ((p,x).pxs) ((q,y).qys)
          = if  p<q  then  (p,x) . join f pxs ((q,y).qys)  else
            if  p>q  then  (q,y) . join f ((p,x).pxs) qys  else
                           (p, f x y) . join f pxs qys
and     join_list f = reduce (join f) []
```

When constructing projections we need to divide type definitions into mutually recursive groups. This reduces to the problem of detecting strongly connected components in a directed graph. The graph is represented as a list of edges and a list of vertices. The algorithm used is a double depth-first search, first on the graph as given, secondly on a reversed version. The complexity is $O(n^2)$, rather than the optimal $O(n)$, so in a realistic system some recoding might be desirable. However, there are many parts of this implementation of partial evaluation where clarity rather than efficiency has been the goal, and where a recoding would provide much greater benefit.

```
and     cyclic es vs = let ins w   = [x ;; (x,y) <- es; y=w]
```

```
                        and outs w = [y ;; (x,y) <- es; x=w]
                            in
                 snd (span ins ([],[]) (snd (dfs outs ([],[]) vs)))


and      dfs r (vs,ns)   []   = (vs,ns)
||       dfs r (vs,ns) (x.xs) = if member vs x then dfs r (vs,ns) xs else
                                  let (vs',ns') = dfs r (x.vs,[]) (r x)
                                  in   dfs r (vs',x.ns'@ns) xs


and      span r (vs,ns)   []   = (vs,ns)
||       span r (vs,ns) (x.xs) = if member vs x then span r (vs,ns) xs else
                                   let (vs',ns') = dfs r (x.vs,[]) (r x)
                                   in   span r (vs',(x.ns').ns) xs
```

The YN type allows conditional responses. The major means of combining these is through the use of ~~~.

```
and
type     YN *a *b = N *a + Y *b


and      (N w) ~~~ f = N w
||       (Y x) ~~~ f = f x


and      lookupYN    []      y = N (y @ " not found")
||       lookupYN ((x,v).xvs) y = if x=y then Y v else lookupYN xvs y


and      AppendYN xs = listYN xs ~~~ (\ys. Y (conc ys))


--       listYN :: List (YN a b) -> YN a (List b)
and      listYN  [] = Y []
||       listYN (x.xs) = addYN x (listYN xs)
and      addYN (N y)  any   = N y
||       addYN (Y x) (N y)  = N y
||       addYN (Y x) (Y xs) = Y (x.xs)
end
```

D.2   Parsing Primitives

In order to provide an acceptable front end for PEL programs a parser is required. This section contains the primitives used to construct it. The technique is described in [Wad85] and [FL89].

```
module  -- PARSELIB.M
#include "library.t"
infixr "!!";            -- 'orelse', corresponds to | in BNF
infixr "..";            -- 'then', BNF uses a space
infixr "x..";           -- 'then', dropping the left hand value
infixr "..x";           -- 'then', dropping the right hand value
infixr ".sep_by.";      --  returns a list delimited by the given separators
infix ".as.";           --  applies semantic functions


export  !! , .. , x.. , ..x , .as. , succeed,
        opt, many, some, .sep_by. , sat, skip, lit;

rec     p1 !! p2 = \inp . p1 inp @ p2 inp
and     p1 .. p2 = \inp . [((v,w),inp'');; (v,inp')<-p1 inp; (w,inp'')<-p2 inp']
and     p x.. q = p .. q  .as.  snd
and     p ..x q = p .. q  .as.  fst
and     p .as. f = \inp . [(f v, inp');; (v,inp') <- p inp]


and     succeed v = \inp . [(v, inp)]
and     opt p v = \inp . [hd ((p !! succeed v) inp)]


and     many p = opt (p .. many p  .as.  cons) []
and     some p = p .. many p  .as.  cons
and     p .sep_by. q = p .. many (q x.. p) .as. cons


and     sat p (c.l) = if p c then [(c,l)] else []
||      sat p []    = []
and     lit t = sat (\x.t=x)


and     skip x (c.l) = if x=c then [(c,l)] else skip x l
||      skip x []    = [(x,[])]
end
```

Bibliography

[Abr86]   S. Abramsky. *Strictness Analysis and Polymorphic Invariance.* In *Programs as Data Objects*, LNCS 217, 1986.

[Abr88]   S. Abramsky. *Notes on Strictness Analysis for Polymorphic Functions.* Draft paper, 1988.

[AH87]   S. Abramsky and C. Hankin (editors). *Abstract Interpretation of Declarative Languages.* Ellis Horwood, Chichester, England, 1987.

[Aug84]   L. Augustsson. *A Compiler for Lazy ML.* Proceedings of Lisp and Functional Programming Conference, Austin, Texas, 1984.

[Bar88]   G. Barzdin. *Mixed Computation and Compiler Basis.* In [BEJ88], pages 15-26, 1988.

[BD77]   R. Burstall and J. Darlington. *A Transformational System for Developing Recursive Programs.* Journal of the ACM 24, pages 44-67, 1977.

[BD89]   A. Bondorf and O. Danvy. *Automatic Autoprojection for Recursive Equations with Global Variables and Abstract Datatypes.* Unpublished. 1989.

[BE88]   M.A. Bulyonkov and A.P. Ershov. *How do ad-hoc Compiler Constructs Appear in Universal Mixed Computation Processes?.* In [BEJ88], pages 65-82, 1988.

[BEJ88]   D. Bjørner, A.P. Ershov and N.D. Jones (Editors). *Partial Evaluation and Mixed Computation.* Proceedings IFIP TC2 Workshop, Gammel Avernæs, Denmark, October 1987. North-Holland, 1988.

[BFSS87]   E.S. Bainbridge, P.J. Freyd, A. Scedrov, and P.J. Scott. *Functorial Polymorphism.* In *Logical Foundations of Functional Programming*, Austin, Texas, 1987, editor G. Huet. Addison-Wesley, 1989.

[BHOS76]   L. Beckman, A. Haraldson, Ö. Oskarsson and E. Sandewall. *A Partial Evaluator, and Its Use as a Programming Tool.* Artificial Intelligence, Vol. 7, No. 4, pages 319-357, 1976.

[BM75]   R. Boyer and J.S. Moore. *Proving Theorems about LISP Functions.* 3rd International Joint Conference on Artificial Intelligence, Stanford Research Institute, Stanford, CA, 1975.

[Bon88]   A. Bondorf. *Towards A Self-Applicable Partial Evaluator for Term Rewriting Systems.* In [BEJ88], pages 27-50, 1988.

[Bon89]   A. Bondorf. *A Self-Applicable Partial Evaluator for Term Rewriting Systems.* In TAPSOFT 89, editors J. Diaz and F. Orejas. LNCS 352, pages 81-95, 1989.

[Bul88]   M.A. Bulyonkov. *A Theoretical Approach to Polyvariant Mixed Computation.* In [BEJ88], pages 51-64, 1988.

[BW88]   R. Bird and P. Wadler. *Introduction to Functional Programming.* Series in Computer Science, editor C.A.R. Hoare, Prentice Hall, 1988.

[CD89]   C. Consel and O. Danvy. *Partial Evaluation of Pattern Matching in Strings.* Inf. Proc. Lett. 30, pages 79-86, 1989.

[CGW87]   T. Coquand, C. Gunter, and G. Winskel. *Domain Theoretic Models of Polymorphism.* Technical Report 116, University of Cambridge, 1987.

[DB75]   J. Darlington and R. Burstall. *A System which Automatically Improves Programs.* 3rd International Joint Conference on Artificial Intelligence, Stanford Research Institute, Stanford, CA, 1975.

[EH80]   P. Emanuelson and A. Haraldsson. *On Compiling Embedded Languages in Lisp.* Proceedings of the 1980 Lisp Conference, Stanford, California, pages 208-215, 1980.

[Ersh82]   A.P. Ershov. *Mixed Computation: Potential Applications and Problems for Study.* Theoretical Computer Science, Vol. 18, pages 41-67, 1982.

[FA88]   D.A. Fuller and S. Abramsky. *Mixed Computation of Prolog Programs.* New Generation Computing, Vol. 6, No. 2,3, pages 119-141, 1988.

[FGSS88]   P.J. Freyd, J.Y. Girard, A. Scedrov, and P.J. Scott. *Semantic Parametricity in Polymorphic Lambda Calculus.* In 3rd Annual Symposium on Logic in Computer Science, Edinburgh, Scotland, 1988.

[FL89]   R. Frost and J. Launchbury. *Constructing Natural Language Interpreters in a Functional Language.* Journal of the British Computer Society, April, 1989.

[FN88]   Y. Futamura and K. Nogi. *Generalized Partial Computation.* In [BEJ88], pages 133-151, 1988.

[Fut71]   Y. Futamura. *Partial Evaluation of Computation Process—An Approach to a Compiler-Compiler.* Systems, Computers, Controls, Vol. 2, No. 5, pages 45-50, 1971.

[Fut83]   Y. Futamura. *Partial Computation of Programs.* In *RIMS Symposia on Software Science and Engineering, Kyoto, Japan, 1982.* Editors E. Goto, et al. LNCS 147, pages 1-35, 1983.

[GJ89]   C.K. Gomard and N.D. Jones. *Compiler Generation by Partial Evaluation: A Case Study.* Information Processing 89, editor H. Gallaire, IFIP, 1989.

[Gom89]   C.K. Gomard. *Higher Order Partial Evaluation—Hope for the Lambda Calculus.* Master's Thesis, DIKU, University of Copenhagen, 1989.

[Hug87]   R.J.M. Hughes. *Analysing Strictness by Abstract Interpretation of Continuations.* In [AH87], pages 63-102, 1987.

[Hug88]   R.J.M. Hughes. *Backwards Analysis of Functional Programs.* In [BEJ88], pages 187-208, 1988.

[Hug89a]   R.J.M. Hughes. *Abstract Interpretation of First Order Polymorphic Functions.* Proceedings of the 1988 Glasgow Workshop on Functional Programming, Research Report 89/R4, University of Glasgow, 1989.

[Hug89b]   R.J.M. Hughes. *Projections for Polymorphic Strictness Analysis.* In *Category Theory in Computer Science,* Manchester, 1989.

[JM86]   N.D. Jones and A. Mycroft. *Data Flow Analysis of Applicative Programs Using Minimal Function Graphs.* Proceedings of the Thirteenth ACM Symposium on Principles of Programming Languages, St. Petersburg, Florida, pages 296-306, 1986.

[Jon88]   N.D. Jones. *Automatic Program Specialization: A Re-Examination from Basic Principles.* In [BEJ88], pages 225-282, 1988.

[JSS85] N.D. Jones, P. Sestoft and H. Søndergaard. *An Experiment in Partial Evaluation: The Generation of a Compiler Generator.* In *Rewriting Techniques and Applications*, editor J.-P. Jouannaud, LNCS 202, pages 124-140, 1985.

[JSS89] N.D. Jones, P. Sestoft and H. Søndergaard. *Mix: A Self-Applicable Partial Evaluator for Experiments in Compiler Generation.* Lisp and Symbolic Computation, 2, pages 9-50, 1989.

[Kur88] P. Kursawe. *Pure Partial Evaluation and Instantiation.* In [BEJ88], pages 283-298, 1988.

[Lau88] J. Launchbury. *Projections for Specialisation.* In [BEJ88], pages 299-315, 1988.

[LR64]   L.A.Lombardi and B.Raphael. *Lisp as the Language for an Incremental Computer.* In *The Programming Language Lisp: Its Operation and Applications*, editors E.C. Berkeley and D.G. Bobrow, pages 204-219, MIT Press, 1964.

[LS87]   J.W. Lloyd and J.C. Shepherdson. *Partial Evaluation in Logic Programming.* Technical Report CS-87-09, University of Bristol, England, 1987.

[Mar80] P. Martin-Löf. *Intuitionistic Type Theory.* Bibliopolis, 1980.

[Mil78] R. Milner. *A theory of type polymorphism in programming.* JCSS 17, pages 348-375, 1978.

[Mog86] T. Mogensen. *The Application of Partial Evaluation to Ray-Tracing.* Master's Thesis, DIKU, University of Copenhagen, 1986.

[Mog88] T. Mogensen. *Partially Static Structures in a Self-Applicable Partial Evaluator.* In [BEJ88], pages 325–347, 1988.

[Mog89] T. Mogensen. *Binding Time Aspects of Partial Evaluation.* Ph.D. Thesis, DIKU, University of Copenhagen, 1989.

[Mos79] P.D. Mosses. *SIS—Semantics Implementation System, Reference Manual and User Guide.* DAIMI Report, MD-30, University of Århus, Denmark, 1979.

[MW87]   P.D. Mosses and D.A. Watt. *The use of action semantics.* In *Formal Description of Programming Concepts III*, editor M. Wirsing, pages 135-163, North-Holland, 1987.

[Myc81]   A. Mycroft. *Abstract Interpretation and Optimizing Transformations for Applicative Programs*. Ph.D. Thesis, University of Edinburgh, 1981.

[Nie88]   F. Nielson. *A Formal Type System for Comparing Partial Evaluators*. In [BEJ88], pages 349-384, 1988.

[Ost88]   B.N. Ostrovsky. *Implementation of Controlled Mixed Computation in System for Automatic Development of Language-Oriented Parsers*. In [BEJ88], pages 385-403, 1988.

[Pier88]   B. Pierce. *A Taste of Category Theory for Computer Scientists*. Research Report CMU-CS-88-203, Carnegie Mellon University, 1988.

[Plo78]   G.D. Plotkin. *Complete Partial Orders, a Tool for Making Meanings*. Lecture notes for the Pisa Summerschool, 1978.

[RB88]   D.E. Rydeheard and R.M. Burstall. *Computational Category Theory*. Series in Computer Science, editor C.A.R. Hoare, Prentice Hall, 1988.

[Rey74]   J.C. Reynolds. *Towards a Theory of Type Structure*. In the proceedings of the *Colloque sur la Programmation*, editor B. Robinet, LNCS 19, 1974.

[Rom88]   S.A. Romanenko. *A Compiler Generator Produced by a Self-Applicable Specializer Can Have a Surprisingly Natural and Understandable Structure*. In [BEJ88], pages 445-463, 1988.

[RT89]   T. Reps and T. Teitelbaum. *The Synthesizer Generator: A System for Constructing Language-Based Editors*. Springer-Verlag, 1989.

[Sch86]   D.A. Schmidt. *Denotational Semantics*. Allyn and Bacon, Inc. Massachusetts, 1986.

[Sch88]   D.A. Schmidt. *Static Properties of Partial Evaluation*. In [BEJ88], pages 465-483, 1988.

[Sco76]   D. Scott. *Data Types as Lattices*. SIAM Journal of Computing, Vol. 5, No. 3, 1976.

[Ses86]   P. Sestoft. *The Structure of a Self-Applicable Partial Evaluator*. In *Programs as Data Objects*, editors H. Ganzinger and N.D. Jones, LNCS 217, pages 236-256, 1986.

[Ses88]   P. Sestoft. *Automatic Call Unfolding in a Partial Evaluator*. In [BEJ88], pages 485-506, 1988.

[Str67]   C. Strachey. *Fundamental Concepts in Programming Languages.* Lecture Notes, International Summer School in Computer Programming, Copenhagen, 1967.

[Tof84]   M. Tofte. *Compiler Generators—What They Can Do, What They Might Do, and What They Will Probably Never Do.* Master's Thesis, DIKU, University of Copenhagen, 1984.

[Tur79]   V.F. Turchin. *A Supercompiler System Based on the Language Refal.* SIGPLAN Notices, Vol. 14, No. 2, pages 46-54, 1979.

[Tur86]   V.F. Turchin. *The Concept of a Supercompiler.* ACM TOPLAS, Vol. 8, No. 3, pages 292-325, 1986.

[Wad85]   P. Wadler. *How to Replace Failure by a List of Successes.* FPCA 85, LNCS 201, 1985.

[Wad88]   P. Wadler. *Deforestation: Transforming Programs to Eliminate Trees.* ESOP 88, LNCS 300, 1988.

[Wad89]   P. Wadler. *Theorems for Free!* FPCA 89, Imperial College, London, 1989.

[WB89]   P. Wadler and S. Blott. *How To Make Ad-hoc Polymorphism Less Ad-hoc.* POPL 89, Austin, 1989.

[WH87]   P. Wadler and R.J.M. Hughes. *Projections for Strictness Analysis.* FPCA 87, Portland, Oregon, 1987.

Index